MMA SCIENCE

A Training, Coaching, and Belt Ranking Guide

PAUL GAVONI

DAVID ZITNICK

ROGER KRAHL

W. ALEX EDMONDS

About MMA Science, Inc

Bringing Tradition, Organization, and Science to Mixed Martial Arts Across the World. Welcome to MMA Science. With more than a combined 75 years of Martial Arts and Combat Sports training, we are very excited to introduce tradition, organization, and science to MMA by bringing you the first ever International Mixed Martial Arts Ranking System. To develop this comprehensive yet easy to follow system, we've spent thousands of hours painstakingly studying and identifying the most common techniques used in MMA and breaking each technique down into a precise and detailed description. In addition, we've identified and broken down fundamental movements so that all students develop critical habits related to any technique.

Copyright © 2020 MMA Science, Inc.

www.mmascience.com

All rights reserved. This book or any portion thereof may not be reproduced or used in any manner whatsoever without the express written permission of the publisher except for the use of brief quotations in a book review.

Printed in the United States of America First Printing, 2020

Supported by Bueno Ventures Management Services, Inc., and 305 Publishing, Inc.

Miami, Florida, USA.

ISBN: 978-1-7359034-0-8

ACKNOWLEDGEMENTS

Between the four of us, we would need to write an entire separate book to truly acknowledge the countless individuals who have contributed to our growth as individuals, martial artists, instructors, and coaches. From family, friends, and students, to fighters, colleagues, editors, and publishers, we are eternally grateful. Thank you to Dr. Kevin Polk, Lauren Haley, Nick Green, Jason Burgos, and Francisco Gomez for your direct contributions.

Writing a book is a challenging endeavor, but we truly wanted to share our collective knowledge learned through a combined century of formal and informal education to help you along in your journey. And we say informal, we mean the University of Hard Knocks where we often learned the hard way. We've made many mistakes along the way, but we've always sought to learn from each of them. This book represents much of what we have learned as the result of our many stumbles and falls in the hopes that you will stumble and fall far less than we have.

Paul, Dave, Roger and Alex

CONTENTS

- ACKNOWLEDGEMENTS 3
- INTRODUCTION 1
  - The Evolution of a Sport and Martial Art 4
  - I Promise Teach, You Promise Learn 7
  - Deliberate Practice 12
  - Behavior Skills Training 16
  - How to Use the MMA Science Task Analysis 18
  - Good Coaching 22
  - Deliberate Coaching 25
  - Using Data to Accelerate Performance 30
  - Using the Performance Evaluation Sheet 32
  - Styles Make Fights 37
  - The Psychology of the Fighter 41
  - Overcoming Fear and Anxiety 48
  - Caring for the Body to Improve Performance 55
  - Final Thoughts 61

SKILL ANALYSIS & PERFORMANCE SCORECARDS 63
  - YELLOW BELT 65
  - ORANGE BELT 107
  - GREEN BELT 139

REFERENCES 173

INTRODUCTION

A JOURNEY OF A THOUSAND MILES begins with a single step; you've just taken that first step. We want to thank you for allowing MMA Science to guide you, step by step, through this very personal journey. Becoming a martial artist is a process that can be life changing—it will develop you physically, mentally, and spiritually. Our system will accelerate your learning of the most sophisticated martial art in existence.

Through our program, you will receive the most comprehensive and detailed curriculum ever created in mixed martial arts (MMA). We have applied the science of human behavior to identify and break down the most critical and fundamental techniques that have been successfully applied in MMA and found to significantly accelerate performance across sports (e.g., Allison & Ayllon, 1980; Krukauskas et al., 2017; Luiselli et al., 2011; Stokes et al., 2010). These fundamental approaches to learning and skill refinement will help you as an MMA student or coach to develop a strong base that will accelerate learning and performance that is recognized and memorialized through belt-ranking progression. As you progress, you will be able to use our videos, drills, and task analysis skill sheets to objectively measure and accelerate skill development. Whether you are seeking to enhance your own development through self-training and self-coaching, or you are an instructor using the program to train and coach others, our system cuts right to the heart of the matter: it teaches you how to automatically apply the right MMA technique in precisely the right way at exactly the right time.

An old Chinese proverb reminds us that "it is better to be a warrior in a garden than a gardener in a war." Whether you would like to develop yourself as a mixed martial artist to become a combat sports athlete or for personal reasons beyond skill development, we recommend you seek to learn about and develop the behaviors associated with the virtues of Bushido, or the way of the warrior. These include the following:

- Justice
- Courage
- Benevolence
- Respect
- Honesty
- Honor
- Loyalty

> *"My code of life and my personal bushido is honor, respect, loyalty, courage and surrender."*
>
> — Rickson Gracie

Tradition

While aspects of developing and passing on Bushido have been absent from MMA as it is seen as a sport, we will make the point in the next section that mixed martial arts has evolved into its own martial arts style. However, because it is such a new martial art, "tradition" has yet to be established in MMA. According to Lexico, *tradition* is "the transmission of customs or beliefs from generation to generation, or the fact of being passed on in this way." For the first two decades in the evolution of MMA, one would be hard pressed to find elements of tradition across the gym. Bowing is a good example of this. Relegated to the traditional martial arts of karate, kung fu, judo, and jiu-jitsu, bowing is absent from some of the primary arts that make up MMA, such as wrestling and boxing. Opponents might be observed demonstrating respect in various ways, such bumping gloves or shaking hands before a match, but those behaviors aren't necessarily associated with customs or beliefs being passed down from generation to generation. In fact, MMA is so relatively new that it's only just experiencing what might be considered the third generation of mixed martial artists. As such, most if not all of the traditions passed on are related to other martial arts. And there are some good traditions, such as bowing, that have evolved and are standard to many arts. Globally, bowing has many different meanings, and different cultures traditionally bow to each other for varied reasons. Tradition, however, isn't the function of bowing. Though only a small physical motion, bowing represents important elements of the Bushido Code, such as integrity, honor, respect, and self-control. Given that MMA is its own martial art, MMA Science recommends MMA gyms embed bowing into the gym culture. For example, there are a few common scenarios where bowing should regularly occur.

> *The supreme art of war is to subdue the enemy without fighting.*
> --
> - Sun Tzu

These scenarios include bowing to the mat prior to training, bowing to training partners on the mat, and bowing to the instructor before and after a class. In these examples, the mixed martial artist is demonstrating respect and humility to the gym and all who are in it. The act of bowing shows they are ready to be a good student and good training partner—one who is open-minded and focused on learning with integrity and safety in mind. As a model for their students, MMA instructors should bow back to their students to reciprocate respect and humility. Good MMA instructors understand there will always be something to learn from their students. It may be directly related to practicing martial arts or perhaps to living the Bushido Code every day outside the gym.

MMA Science contends that bowing in the gym is a tradition that should be embraced across MMA gyms. Good coaches connect lessons learned in the MMA gym to everyday life outside the gym walls. Bowing is a reminder of lessons that the mixed martial artist should regularly discuss and practice, such as respect and self-control.

INTRODUCTION

It is our greatest hope that you will use the knowledge and skills gained from MMA to be a peaceful warrior—one who not only seeks self-development but also supports the development of others. Enjoy your journey as you evolve mentally and physically as a result of the challenges you will face and overcome on the mats and throughout your life as a mixed martial artist. And welcome to MMA Science.

THE EVOLUTION OF A SPORT *AND* MARTIAL ART

> *It is not the strongest of the species that survives,*
> *nor the most intelligent, but the one most responsive to change.*
> --
> - Charles Darwin

If you have been a fan of MMA since its inception, you've had a front row seat to its birth and evolution for the past quarter century. With lineage that can be traced back almost 3,000 years ago to the Greek Olympic sport Pankration (Georgiou, 2008), MMA is considered by many to be the most sophisticated martial art in the world. Much like the natural selection process underlying evolution, long-time MMA fans have witnessed different forms of the martial arts reign during certain eras. Mixed martial artists such as Royce Gracie, Randy Couture, Chuck Liddell, Wanderlei Silva, and Anderson Silva all dominated with strategies heavily focused in BJJ, wrestling, kickboxing, and Muay Thai. Since that time, MMA has evolved into its own sport and martial art, one that is separate from those and other individual disciplines of martial arts. Those disciplines are certainly all major components that must be mastered; however, they must be mastered in their respective MMA variations. We compare these disciplines to different dialects of the same language. For example, consider Spanish from Spain vs. from Mexico vs. from Cuba—they are all the same language but have variations that can make communication between the three very difficult. Similarly, the major components of MMA must be trained in their MMA variations if mixed martial artists wish to compete at high levels or master MMA as a self-defense. While some might argue that MMA is a sport, we suggest that it is a highly effective martial art that can be easily used for self-defense. The sport of MMA has rules; however, in true self-defense, these rules go out the window. By simply altering the targets (e.g., instead of striking the head, targeting the eyes or the groin) and choosing the appropriate technique for a given self-defense situation, the mixed martial artist is armed with a deadly self-defense repertoire.

In an MMA competition, many variables must be addressed related to components of the striking and grappling arts—components that have evolved since the inception of MMA. That evolution started with Brazilian jiu-jitsu, or BJJ. This mostly unknown art dominated the earliest evolution of MMA. Then was the wrestling era (e.g., Kerr, Coleman, Couture, and Ortiz), where powerful wrestlers won with strong takedowns, positioning, and relentless ground and pound. Then came high-level strikers (e.g., Crocop, Lidell, and Silva). The longer technical knock-out (KO) artist sprawl and brawl mentality gave everyone a new problem.

As a result of these other forefathers, we now have MMA as we know it today. The kids who watched those earlier eras are growing up, and they have taken a piece of all era with them. These kids are also trained at legitimate MMA schools, not BJJ, wrestling, boxing, or kickboxing gyms. In each MMA school, mixed martial artists and coaches work together to improve each major component of the school's MMA variations. Because of this evolution, the martial artist can now specialize in MMA. Indeed, all the major components can be trained under one roof where there are coaches who collaborate to learn about and connect each other's styles; moreover, there are now pure MMA coaches beginning to emerge who have only been trained in MMA. The future of MMA is exciting!

A few great examples of the complete mixed martial artist might be found in Demetrious Johnson, Frankie Edgar, George St Pierre, Cub Swanson, and Jorge Masvidal, just to name a few. While many arts can be added as weapons, to be a well-rounded MMA artist, you must be proficient in striking, wrestling/judo/Thai clinching, and BJJ. These components are fundamental to MMA. They are listed in that order only because that is how a fight typically progresses (i.e., start standing, takedown, ground). Each major component can be broken down into its own individual art. While there are many, MANY martial arts techniques that can be effective under the right conditions, there would be too many to place in one system. However, through our research and experience, we have identified the most frequently used techniques with the highest probability of success in MMA and broken them down throughout our program. But before you venture on, let's take a basic look at how the use of different striking and grappling arts must be varied to be effective within MMA.

The MMA Variation

While different combat sports and martial arts focus on a core skillsets and strategies particular to each discipline, MMA requires its own specific set of skillsets and approaches because of the many offensive and defensive variables that must be considered. Let's take a look at some of the key considerations and variations.

Stance – You must have a hybrid stance of the major components to be able to effectively flow from one aspect of the fight to another. Can you imagine starting an MMA fight in a wrestling stance? You might get kneed or kicked in the head! Individually, each stance has weaknesses and strengths. The strong points of each stance must be put together to develop a functional MMA stance.

Striking – Mixed martial artists must be prepared to wrestle and clinch very often. They must also maintain distances with not only their jabs but also their kicks. They must understand the difference in these distances and be acutely aware of what offense or defense works at varying ranges. Distance management in MMA is drastically different than it is striking arts such as boxing and kickboxing where takedowns are not a threat. At times, for instance, you as a mixed martial artist or coach must adjust striking distance when attempting to step up a takedown using striking.

Wrestling/clinching/judo – Without some level of striking that allows mixed martial artists to achieve these positions, modern-day MMA would be all but impossible. Even expert BJJ practitioners like the Gracie fighters in the earliest MMA events used limited striking to close the distance for takedowns. No matter how limited a mixed martial artist's striking, it must be good enough to safely close the distance for a clinch or takedown. Legendary wrestler Steve Mocco listed major changes that should be considered when using wrestling in MMA. They are as follows:

1. MMA requires striking to set up takedowns and defend against opponents striking while trying to close the distance. In regular wrestling, the position and defense of your hips are most important.

2. Wrestling is about scoring points. MMA wrestling is about neutralizing your opponent and limiting the damage they can do to you.

3. You can be out of bounds in wrestling, causing a break in action. MMA obviously does not have this, and MMA wrestlers must be able to continuously wrestle. The cage in MMA also causes many of its own difficulties, both offensively and defensively.

Brazilian jiu-jitsu – In MMA, BJJ components focus on top control, position, ground and pound, and submissions. There are no collars/sleeves to grab. Sport BJJ often entails pulling guard and working from a deep half guard. And under these conditions, that approach is very effective. In MMA, however, this is often a poor choice to make. Moreover, it could cost the mixed martial artist the fight in competition, or perhaps their life in a street fight where the wrong technique (e.g., using a triangle from the guard) might be exploited and used against them (e.g., if caught in a triangle, the mixed martial artist being picked up and having their head slammed down onto the concrete). In MMA, the attacks must change, and the urgency to get off your back must be a high priority. The pace of MMA grappling is much higher, so the mixed martial artist must get used to this speed. And in competition, they must get used to the cage as it can be effectively leveraged by the savvy mixed martial artist.

Ground and pound – Ground and pound, as termed by Mark "The Hammer" Coleman, was a game changer. This alone can make or break the BJJ expert's game in mixed martial arts. Those who use basic striking techniques and secure a dominant top position in MMA can use ground and pound to set up a variety of submissions. Or in some cases, they might simply use their BJJ expertise to secure and maintain a position where they engage in ground and pound to finish the fight.

I PROMISE TEACH, YOU PROMISE LEARN

For many, *The Karate Kid* could be considered the *Rocky* of martial arts. Brimming with literal and metaphorical life lessons, *The Karate Kid* highlights many lessons that can be applied to MMA. Among these lessons are gems related to the shared responsibility of coaches and mixed martial artists. Mr. Miyagi illustrated this responsibility well when he declared, "First make sacred pact. I promise teach karate. That my part. You promise learn. I say, you do, no questions. That your part." While his words are wise in the sense that they clarify the shared responsibility in the relationship, they are just the tip of the iceberg in terms of the actual complexity involved in coaching and learning.

In fact, many believe the coach/mixed martial artist relationship is solely based on Mr. Miyagi's simple formula. That is, the coach tells the mixed martial artist what to do, and the mixed martial artist does it. If only it were that easy. In reality, there is a science behind coaching and learning. Though most of the greatest coaches were not formerly trained in the science of coaching, they are likely great observers of their own coaching behavior, the coaching behavior of others, and the impact of their coaching behavior on mixed martial artists. Professors in their own right, such coaches have become purveyors of the sweet science of MMA.

> *The capacity to learn is a gift; the ability to learn is a skill; the willingness to learn is a choice.*
>
> --
>
> - Brian Herbert

Similarly, great mixed martial artists tend to be good observers of their own behavior (e.g., noticing the smallest change in their guard), how their behavior impacts an opponent's behavior (e.g., an opponent may throw fewer right hands when the lead hand is kept high in their guard), and how an opponent's behavior impacts the MMA artist's own behavior (e.g., a certain offense evokes a particular defense).

If you have a strong work ethic and are like the mixed martial artists described above, you likely excel at your craft. If you do not, there are some things you might consider for accelerating your performance or, in the case of the coach, the performance of others. In the next sections, we will reflect on some high-impact behaviors associated with being a good coach and a good student.

The Coach

Despite Mr. Miyagi's suggestion, coaching should be more than "I say, you do." Both the MMA coach and MMA student should have a basic understanding of coaching and learning to engage in the pinpointed behaviors associated with knowledge, skill, and performance development. This process involves using instructional design (Johnson & Chase, 1981) to develop and follow a very specific sequence that includes establishing objectives, analyzing the task, determining standards, assessing a mixed martial artist's current repertoire, engaging in behavior skills training, and using behavioral coaching. While many great coaches understand and apply these processes using various sequences and terminology, the following points reflect the essence of coaching in relation to both skill development and the transfer of those skills into actual combat.

Objective

The goal of a coach should be to bring out the best in the mixed martial artist. For this to happen, there must be focused objectives (sub-goals, if you will) that lead the MMA artist to desired outcomes. Some might think "winning" should always be the objective, but it shouldn't. Objectives can be strategically aligned with ideal performance that can lead to the ultimate long-term goal of winning, but they shouldn't be listed as "winning." Why not? It doesn't provide the coach and mixed martial artist with direction. It's like saying you are going on vacation but haven't figured out where you're going or determining how you will get there. Plus, if the competitive mixed martial artist is always focused on winning, they're not focused on what is required to win—specifically, they're not focused on developing and executing the right skills in the right way at the right time.

Breaking It Down

One of the primary functions of a coach should be to break down complex tasks into chunks that can be easily practiced, thus helping the mixed martial artist move closer to an objective. In the behavior sciences, this is known as a task analysis. For example, if the objective is improving defense through increased and specific head movement, then a task analysis might break that head movement down into very precise steps that a mixed martial artist can follow, similar to the way we've handled the task analysis within this manual. The less skilled the mixed martial artist is in a particular area, the more detailed the steps should be. The trick here is targeting the right skills to practice, which requires understanding the difference between fundamental, component, and composite skills. While MMA Science has done all of the foot work for you in this manual, there may be other techniques not covered here that the coach might wish to teach or the student might wish to learn.

Fundamental Skills

"Wax on, wax off" was the mantra repeated by Mr. Miyagi in *The Karate Kid*. What Mr. Miyagi understood very well was that his student needed to develop fundamental skills before learning more complex skills. The fundamentals are prerequisites for all other learning, and sometimes the task analysis must be broken down into these "micro behaviors," if you will. Much like an arrow being shot by the archer, if fundamental skills are initially off in even the slightest at the beginning, they will ultimately fall far short of hitting the bullseye. In other words, if fundamental skills are not in place, everything else is impacted. For example, a fundamental skill might be having the appropriate fight stance, or effectively distributing and shifting weight between combos. Too much weight in the wrong direction can affect performance in virtually every other area.

Unfortunately, though fundamental skills are by far the most important aspect of training that should receive deliberate practice, they are typically not trained to fluency, to the detriment of the mixed martial artist (more on deliberate practice and fluency shortly). Working on fundamentals is not "sexy," so to speak. It doesn't look cool, and it might suggest to some that the mixed martial artist or coach is somehow "less than" because they're not focusing on composite skills that make up exotic combinations. Mixed martial artists or coaches who are less confident may opt to focus on the "show" combos instead of the "grow" fundamentals.

The concept of accelerating performance by focusing on fundamentals was illustrated well in research related to teaching elementary students to read. In this research, the investigator found that, by blending (think sounding out letters to make words) only 40 or so letter–sound combinations in the English language, a child will be able to read almost 500,000 words (Alessi, 1987). Can you imagine the time saved teaching the 40 sounds compared with teaching 500,000 words?

The same concept applies to MMA. Coaches who focus on developing fundamental skills exponentially multiply their mixed martial artist's ability to learn and apply more complex skills in the future. Examples of fundamental skills include the following:

- Posture
- Stance
- Weight distribution
- Core rotation
- Weight shifting
- Linear and lateral movement
- Proper guard
- Arm extension
- Fist rotation

Ironically, if coaches and mixed martial artists focus on developing fundamental skills to fluency when teaching a new skill, not only do the MMA artists' skills and performance develop at an accelerated rate, but the artists can actually learn far more and spontaneously develop their own skills …even in the absence of coaching. And this truth isn't reserved for new or green mixed martial artists. It's applicable to mixed martial artists at the highest level of the game. While many are successful despite flaws in their fundamentals, we will never know how many potential world champions came up short simply because of only the slightest flaw in a fundamental. Such flaws become progressively magnified as mixed martial artists climb the rankings in MMA.

Component Skills

Where fundamental skills are the building blocks of component skills, component skills are the building blocks of composite skills, which make up complex offensive and defensive combinations. Component skills are a combination of fundamental skills that make up any one skill. Some examples of component skills in striking include, but are not limited to:

- Straight punches
- Hooks
- Uppercuts
- Catching punches with arms/fists
- Rolling under a punch
- Slipping a punch

Good coaches know that it doesn't make sense to focus on a combination involving the straight right-hook if the fighter is unable to throw either punch correctly. In other words, you have to walk before you run.

Composite Skills

Composite skills are the mix and match of component skills. This is essentially chaining skills together. For example, three-punch combinations might be made up of a jab, hook, and uppercut, which are three component skills of striking. If any fundamental or component skill is lacking, the fighter will begin building bad habits. Remember, practice doesn't make perfect…perfect practice makes perfect.

Standard

Coaches and fighters should know what constitutes mastery of the objective in terms of what the skill actually looks like, and what outcome can be expected if the skills are performed correctly. This should first involve effectively performing the skill under practice conditions, then progressively moving towards performing the skill under sparring, and then fight conditions. It takes years of diligence and practice.

Fighter Repertoire

Determining the fighter's repertoire simply means figuring how what the fighter actually is bringing to the table in comparison to the established standard. That is, what does the coach have to start with? If improved defense was the objective, and head movement was the skill being focused on, how well is a fighter able to perform head movement in practice or during live sparring? And do they possess the self-efficacy (think confidence in their ability) to actually apply specific skills in a fight.

It's important to differentiate between these because sometimes it's not just about the fighter knowing what to do, but more about knowing when to do it. And when it comes to skills development, many times it's actually about a fighter's self-efficacy as this drives the fighter's attempts at applying the skill in an actual fight.

In terms of the "when" or what educators might call conditional knowledge, it is the difference between Anderson Silva dropping his hands against Demian Maia—in hopes of drawing in an attack—and doing the same against Chris Weidman. Just knowing how to do it is not the end of the process. The mixed martial artist needs to know precisely what to do, precisely how to do it, and then execute the technique at precisely the right moment.

A Masterpiece at Work

Like the building of a house, building a fighter's skill-set is a long and repetitive brick-by-brick undertaking. Fighters who can pull-off new moves in the middle of a fight are the outliers; however, there ability to do so is still rooted in a strong foundation. There are far less Mark Zuckerberg's (where success comes quickly) and far more Steve Jobs' (where success is built off of victories and failures over time) in the fight game.

> *"Repetition is the mother of skill."*
> --
> Tony Robbins

These techniques for building skills are processes that have also been cultivated over generations by some of the great minds in performance improvement, and existing research proves its value. Fundamentals are the foundation and beams that a fighter's techniques are built upon. Component skills are the brick and mortar that solidify it all. Composite skills are like the elevators, stairs, doors and rooms that make the building come to life. But just knowing how to build skills isn't enough. The mixed martial artist must learn to perfect the skill.

DELIBERATE PRACTICE

While fundamental skills are the building blocks of component skills, component skills are the building blocks of composite skills, which make up complex offensive and defensive combinations. But simply knowing the sequence of how something occurs is not enough. The mixed martial artist must also engage in a training sequence to develop the skill in a way that will successfully generalize from drilling to actual combat. The ultimate goal should be to become an expert at being a mixed martial artist. But to become an expert, there are skills on top of skills one needs to acquire beyond the basic striking, grappling, and defending techniques required to make it as a mixed martial artist. We've seen mixed martial artists who are specialists and experts in one area, such as kickboxing or wrestling, but even then, it's typically not enough. Skills on top of skills is what is required. However, trying to tackle the skills-on-top-of-skills approach can be overwhelming. Therefore, it's important to identify the skills within a skill, one skill, and focus only on that. The most optimal and efficient way to achieve proficiency and potential expert status in one particular skill is to engage in deliberate practice. In fact, we'd argue it's the only way.

Deliberate practice and the amount of time devoted to it are what researchers in the sport sciences believe differentiates the experts from the non-experts, the elites from the non-elites, and the professionals from the amateurs. Deliberate practice is not a simple concept of just getting in the gym and working out longer and harder. Rather, deliberate practice is a systematic approach to the art of developing a skill. It is precise and purposeful. Sport psychology consultant and deliberate practice expert Dr. Alex Edmonds reminds us that the general premise of deliberate practice is to break down one specific skill of grappling, for example, and understand all aspects of it. These aspects are broken down into chunks, if you will, and practiced repeatedly until a certain level of proficiency is achieved. The practice is not done in isolation, but achieved over time while receiving a constant stream of reinforcing and corrective feedback from a good coach. In addition, the practice of these skills must be systematically made more challenging over time. That way, the skill of grappling, including all the intricacies within that skill, is slowly developed through repetition and corrective feedback that makes the repetitive task progressively more challenging. Even so, purposely engaging in deliberate practice is easier said than done.

Even if a coach does not understand all the science behind training, great coaches understand that learning is a process. Since repetition is critical to gaining proficiency in any skill, many mixed martial artists fall into the trap of overtraining because they are engaging in too many *physical* repetitions, not realizing that repetitions and learning do not always have to be physical. Training, as a whole, encompasses the idea of both knowledge and skill acquisition. In other words, the mixed martial artist must be able to discriminate between conditions and engage in the right skills in precisely the right way at exactly the right time. *Knowing* what to do, how to do it, and when to do it until it becomes automatic is critical in MMA. Developing automatic and accurate responses doesn't have to be as taxing as the wear and tear that comes from sparring or hard physical training. However, developing this knowing *does* require repetition so that the martial artist can react automatically. Note that it's not just any reps, though. Repetition should include high-quality reps with deliberate focus on a specific skill, the components of this skill, and associated strategies. A key strategy to accelerating skill acquisition and proficiency in a non-physical way is through the process of video modeling and video feedback (Hazen et al., 1990), often referred to as *film study*. An integral approach and component to engaging in deliberate practice, film study has been shown to more than double the performance of athletes who add it to their training package (Boyer et al., 2009).

Integrating film study into the regimen puts the MMA artist one step closer to advancing the non-physical aspect of practice into deliberate practice. Film study is cost-effective and allows for deep analysis because of the practical benefits of using pause, rewind, and slow-motion options. As we mentioned, film study isn't used enough, even by the highest-level fighters in the UFC. But we should be clear: just like when practicing the rear-naked choke, there are optimal and non-optimal ways to integrate film study into a regimen.

Film study can be broken down into three simple categories:
1. Study the experts
2. Study your own fights
3. Study your opponent

Each one of these categories should be studied systematically to get the best out of each. However, not everyone knows exactly what they're looking at in film study. If you don't have the luxury of sitting with an expert coach who can help you break down film footage, then we suggest spending a lot of time in category 1—studying the experts.

Study the Experts

One can learn a new skill by watching others and copying it. Anyone can easily find several clips of a professional executing strikes, submissions, takedowns, and transitions. In addition, there are experts who break down popular fights by showing what the fighters did well and where they failed. After you study these films, we then suggest you set up a camera, grab a practice partner, and record yourself attempting a particular technique. After recording your move, compare it to the professional. Was it similar? What was missing? Make note of what was good, what needs to be improved, and what your practice partner was doing (was it effective for them?).

MMA Science provides mixed martial artists access to detailed videos of each skill and drills that complement the task analyses in this manual so that you can drill and perfect each component of a skill. Remember, MMA coaches and students can use the combination of these resources to accelerate learning and performance. Students can also compare their videos to the standards provided by MMA Science as a means of assessing and improving their own performance.

Study Your Own Performance

Although a mirror can give live feedback on our own behavior, it is rarely possible to look at a mirror while sparring or completing a live drill. An easy fix for this is to video record and study your own sparring sessions and fight films, if available. A good way to study your own performance is to create a form (see example below) for you and your coach to study and review. Have your coach note the various aspects of each fight and note exactly where you're strong, just okay, and poor...and make sure they are specific! Remember, part of deliberate practice is breaking down a specific technique into its components. In this case, not only are you breaking down a technique into its components, but you're doing it to yourself and then adding performance notes. Next, you should watch your own fight to see if you see the same thing the coach saw. This approach will advance your perspective and understanding of your strengths and weaknesses at a level you would not have been able to achieve prior. See the example form below for a visual illustration of what your coach's notes might look like.

	Coach and Fighter		
Level	**Optimal**	**Moderate**	**Poor**
Striking	Defending the left hook using a high guard with the right hand. Using the jab to set up power.	Checking low kicks.	Slipping the right hand while in the pocket. Using strike defense to set up offense.
Notes		Stance was too linear in the pocket, which delayed check response.	Slips occurred, but head was too far off line, which created susceptibility to head kicks. Defended punches well, but did not counter after.

When watching the recording of yourself, slow down the clip and look closely at precisely what you were doing. How were your feet? Did you overextend? Did you exhale while striking? Record yourself again, and repeat the process. Each fighter and coach should be studying the performances without bias. Using this information, you can create a plan for improvement with your coach by digging down into the specific areas. Beyond observing your performance, observe the conditions in which you were more likely to perform optimally, moderately, or poorly. Sometimes poor performance is not skill related, but rather tactical in nature. In other words, fighters may be doing the right thing at the wrong time.

Study Your Opponent

Many competitive mixed martial artists boldly declare, "I don't study my opponent." In some cases, this is simply bravado; in others, it may be true. And sometimes, the fighter who is not studying their opponent may be a good or even great fighter. However, we contend that fighters who neglect this aspect of their development are not reaching their maximum potential. Therefore, we strongly recommend that studying one's opponent be programmed into a fighter's camp. Good fighters can become great, and great fighters can become champions by integrating film study into their deliberate practice routines.

The primary purpose of studying an opponent is to understand then recognize a fighter's tendencies in a fight. Though it's not a perfect solution, understanding a fighter's tendencies allows for predicting their next move, thus increasing the likelihood of an effective response—which then increases your chances of winning. The best way to study your opponent is to create a scouting report for each fight. How? Look for tendencies related to a few broad areas, and then hone in on more specifics. For example, when looking at striking, a simple but critical piece of information is stance. Preparing for a southpaw is vastly different than preparing for an orthodox fighter. More nuanced aspects of striking might be the tendency of the fighter to throw overhands or perhaps even subtle movements like shaking their right hand just prior to throwing it. Another aspect is to gauge the timing and speed of their strikes, for example. This is a potential data point that can be added into a sparring session in preparation for the fight. After observing tendencies, pick two or three to focus on, and then create drills that allow for deliberate practice related to capitalizing on these tendencies.

> *Learning is not the product of teaching.*
> *Learning is the product of the activity of the learners.*
> --
> John Holt

Remember, film study should be considered a major part of practice, not just an adjunct to it or a side note. Treat fighting like a game of chess. Become a student of the game. Be aware that becoming better doesn't just involve physical training—it involves training the mind, too. And that training will ultimately translate to success in the cage, octagon, or ring.

BEHAVIOR SKILLS TRAINING

If you are an MMA Coach seeking to develop your student's skills, or a student being coached, it's important to understand the simple sequence with which developing skills should occur. While many believe that teaching is simply about telling somebody what to do and how to do it, as we've illustrated, it is clearly far more complex than that. Fortunately, the science of human behavior provides a simple yet well-researched process for developing skills that incorporates practical strategies that have been found to accelerate knowledge and skill acquisition (e.g. Quintero, 2018). This process is called behaviors skills training (BST). In short, BST employs instruction, modeling, practice, and feedback as a system for developing a variety of performance skills. Most coaches intuitively use the BST process during their instruction. Here are the steps with a brief explanation for each:

- **Step 1:** Specify the skill being taught. For example, "I am going to teach the right cross today."

- **Step 2:** Provide the MMA student with a written summary of the specific skill. While this is virtually non-existent across most martial arts, MMA Science provides a written summary and precise task analysis that breaks down each technique into its components.

- **Step 3:** Verbally describe the skill with a rationale (the why!) for targeting the skill for training. Good coaches are athletic leaders, and good leaders start with the why to ensure that martial artists are motivated by the end goal. For example, if teaching a martial artist to pivot their rear foot when they throw the cross, a good coach would inform the student of why the pivot is important. In this case, the pivot provides greater range, greater power with the cross, and further loads the hook to generate more power. Understanding the why increases the likelihood that the martial artist will want to perfect this important component of the technique.

- **Step 4:** Physically demonstrate the skill for the mixed martial artists. It makes sense that people need to see what something looks like as a model to strive for. This step is a great place to incorporate video modeling.

- **Step 5:** Observe the mixed martial artists as they practice the targeted skill. Good coaches remain vigilant and record video when possible as they are constantly assessing the martial artist's performance.

- **Step 6:** All learning requires feedback. While constantly assessing targeted skills, good coaches provide corrective or reinforcing feedback to the mixed martial artists based on their performance. This is where the rubber meets the road. They say practice makes perfect. But in fact, practice makes permanent. If a martial artist is incorrectly performing a skill in high repetition, they will eventually become really good at performing a technique that is really bad. This is why it's critical for the coach to provide feedback early and often, especially when a new skill is being learned.

- **Step 7:** This is the final step. Continue steps 4, 5, and 6 until the mixed martial artist can correctly perform the targeted skill. That is, repeatedly provide a quick model of the technique or a component of it, if needed, and then observe and provide feedback to correct and reinforce incremental improvements toward the desired skill until the martial artist can perform independently, without feedback from the coach. A tip for providing feedback is shifting from telling to asking after the martial artist has received ample and specific feedback on the targeted skill. For example, rather than reminding the martial artist to pivot their back foot when they throw the cross, a good coach might ask, "Did you pivot your back foot?" or, "What should you be doing with your back foot when you throw the cross?"

Fluency

The mixed martial artist does not have time to think. They must react quickly and accurately if they are to be effective. While receiving regular feedback from coaches is important (especially during the acquisition of new skills), the martial artist must develop fluency of critical skills if they are going to effectively generalize into actual combat. You can think of *behavioral fluency* as "a fluid combination of accuracy plus speed that characterizes competent performance" (Binder, 1996, p. 164). That is, behavioral fluency is doing the right thing quickly.

> *I fear not the man who has practiced 10,000 kicks once, but I fear the man who has practiced one kick 10,000 times.*
> --
> Bruce Lee

Most people refer to this as something that is "second nature." The skill must also be durable. In other words, it's not enough for somebody to practice something enough until they can accurately perform it. Rather, like with riding a bike, the skill must be engaged in long enough so that it maintains over time. This *fluency training*, as it is known to behavior scientists, adds the important speed criterion so that the mixed martial artist can consistently respond accurately and without hesitation when the opportunity presents itself. This training is a prerequisite for any mixed martial artist if they ever wish to regularly and successfully use the skill under combat conditions.

HOW TO USE THE MMA SCIENCE TASK ANALYSIS

MMA Science is very proud to bring the first-ever belt ranking system to MMA. Through this organized curriculum that builds off the fundamentals, we provide hundreds of step-by-step descriptions, pictures, and videos that allow MMA coaches and students to immediately put our system into action. Moreover, our system provides a simple measurement tool that allows for precise teaching and evaluation during training or belt testing. Using the scientific process of task analysis, we have broken down the most effective techniques commonly used in MMA into components so that they can be easily taught and practiced until a certain level of proficiency is achieved over progressively more challenging conditions. As mentioned earlier, using our program, the martial artist is able to accelerate the development of "fluency," as evidenced by techniques eventually occurring quickly, precisely, and automatically during combat conditions.

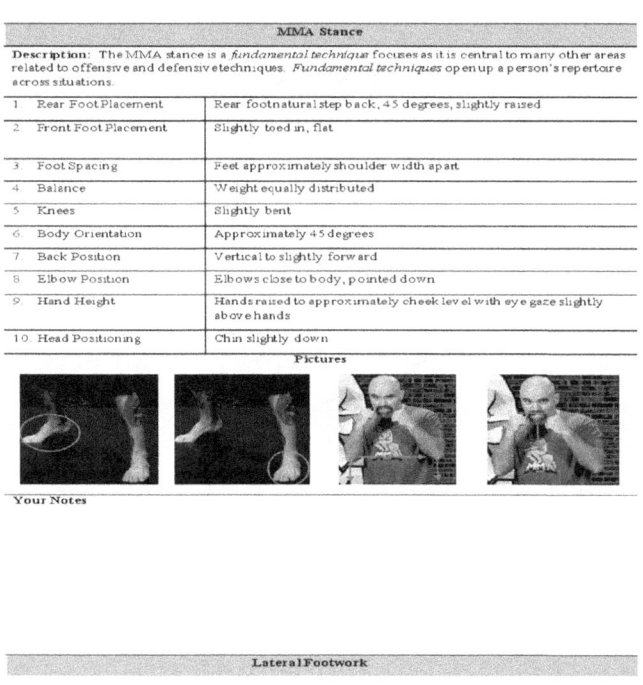

Table 1. Task Analysis Steps.

A task analysis, as illustrated in Table 1, is the process of breaking down a complex skill into a sequence of more manageable steps. Each step in the task analysis is linked together like a chain. It's far too much to teach any martial artist the 10 steps to a new skill all at once. The martial artist is likely to make many errors as they struggle to remember each step. The task analysis provided by MMA Science makes teaching and learning easier as it allows for the details of each step to be taught and mastered before advancing to the next step. When it comes to martial arts, details make the most impact. Defining specific behaviors associated with different skills makes it easier for the coach to measure and provide precise feedback on specific steps of the skill to help shape the martial artist's performance. Similarly, the MMA student can use the task analysis as an aide to guide and measure their own skill development. Having a precise understanding and description of all the steps involved in a particular skill can assist in precisely identifying specific behaviors that require additional instruction, feedback, or practice.

Forward Chaining

Typically, the task analysis will be used to teach and learn a skill using what's called *forward chaining*. With forward chaining, the martial artist starts by focusing on mastery of the first step of the skill. They then move "forward" to the next steps of the skill, then the next, and so on. If the martial artist is struggling with a particular step or sequence of steps, those steps can be isolated, practiced to mastery, and then placed back in the chain to continue building the skill.

While most of the time MMA students will use forward chaining to develop skills by starting from the top and working forward, you can also use *backward chaining*, as we call it in the science, by starting the chain at the bottom and working backward through the task analysis.

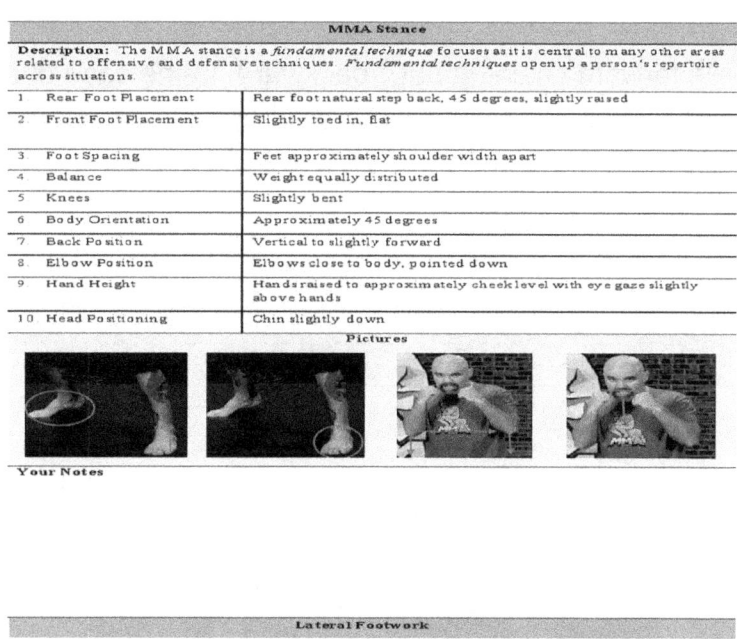

Table 2. Task Analysis Forward Chaining.

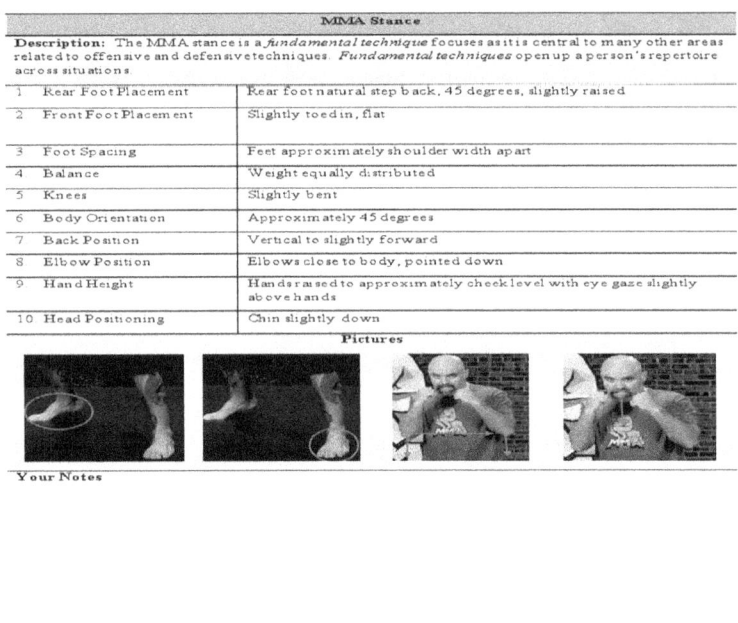

Table 3. Task Analysis Forward Chaining.

Backward Chaining

Backward chaining is like forward chaining but…backward. In the case of the MMA stance as an example, Step 1 would be focused on learning the head positioning, Step 2 would be focused on hand height, and so on.

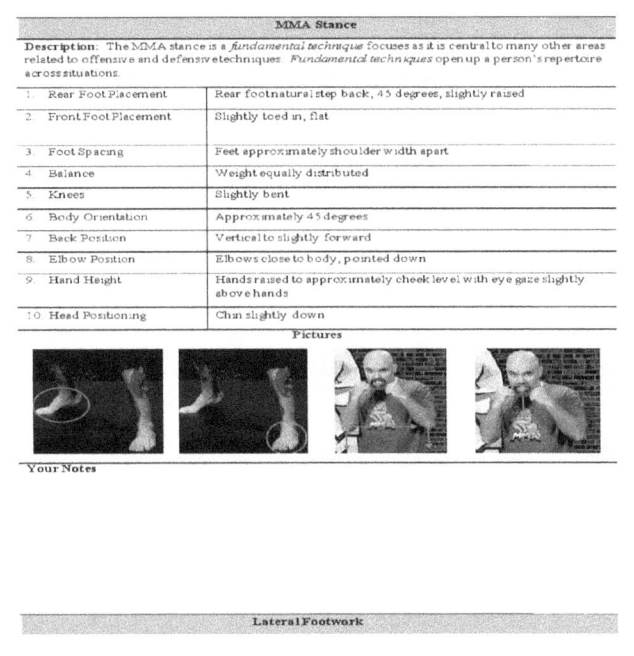

Table 4. Task Analysis Backward Chaining.

Similar to how things work in forward chaining, the martial arts student must properly remember the order of the tasks. If the student achieved mastery in Step 2, but struggles to independently complete Steps 3–7, it's time to go back a few steps.

Forward Chaining vs. Backward Chaining: Which is Better?

There isn't really a clear answer to whether forward or backward chaining is better, but here are some pros and cons to each type.

Forward chaining allows the student to immediately get into a step-by-step sequence. It's like getting an instant win. And it makes more sense to most people. Those are the pros. Meanwhile, the cons of this type of chaining are that the martial artist who is learning a new skill has to progress through all of the steps of a specific skill before achieving the last step, which is typically the most satisfying. For example, the most satisfying step of the arm bar from the mount is typically the completion of the very last step that involves extending the arm and elevating the hips.

In backward chaining, once the martial artist masters the last step, they always finish with it. One of the pros to this is that it can be highly gratifying. Using the example of the arm bar, the first step taught might be focused on what to do when an opponent's arm is fully extended, which requires the martial artist to simply elevate their hips to finish the arm bar. The second step might be extending the arm, then finishing with the elevated hips, and so on. A major con to backward chaining is that it can feel awkward to both the coach and the student as starting from the last step of a technique is not the typical sequence of training.

Whatever the pros and cons, forward and backward chaining can both be powerful tools for accelerating performance. There's no absolute right answer when it comes to forward or backward chaining. Instead, there's a right choice for individual mixed martial arts students when it comes to their own learning history and different techniques (Libby et al., 2008). Just remember that a task analysis allows for chaining, and chaining is a great way to accelerate teaching and learning through precision.

GOOD COACHING

Good coaching can serve to accelerate performance and greatly reduce injury. One study found that having an experienced coach decreases the likelihood of severe injury to players by 50% (Knowles et al., 2009). Even without knowledge of the scientific approach to behavior skills and fluency training, good coaches intuitively know how to progressively build skillsets that will generalize or extend into a real fight. Mixed martial artists need to know what skills a great coach possesses so that the artists know they are being provided the best instruction possible. Good and well-meaning coaches may "tell" their mixed martial artists to do something but are not rewarded with the desired performance during the fight.

> *A good coach will make his players see what they can be rather than what they are.*
> --
> Ara Parseghian

We use the word "tell" instead of "teach" because the real measure of being taught is whether the mixed martial artist learned; consequently, the measure of learning is the mixed martial artist performing the said skill in the fight. If the mixed martial artist did not perform, they may have been "told" the right thing to do, but they were never coached to fluency. Though great coaches don't call it BST, they do regularly engage in the BST process outlined above in their day-to-day instruction. They understand that good training involves instruction, modeling, and rehearsal with feedback to reinforce or "shape" incremental improvements toward a desired skill.

Like when a sculptor molds a piece of clay, shaping is an essential part of coaching, and all good coaches use the process of shaping. Below, the acronym **C-O-A-C-H** is used to illustrate many of the necessary elements of good coaching for developing skills. And remember, this acronym can be used as a self-monitoring and coaching approach. Good coaches, and this includes you coaching yourself, should do the following:

- **Communicate** skillset goals, and structure a variety of systematic drills that allow for deliberate practice. Regularly setting and posting goals has been shown to accelerate performance (Brobst & Ward, 2002). Provide a description of the skill, its importance or rationale, and when and when not to use the skill.
- **Observe** the mixed martial artist under different conditions. In other words, coaches should observe the mixed martial artist shadow boxing, hitting the bag, sparring, etc.
- **Affirm** by providing detailed and immediate feedback (Miltenberger, 2008) to the mixed martial artist when they perform the skill (or parts of the skill) as intended. Coaches should strive to use a strength-based perspective for emerging skills, with the rule of thumb being

to recognize what the mixed martial artist is doing right twice as much compared to what they are not doing. For example, "Johnny, you pivoted nicely on your back foot when you threw your cross. This gives you greater range and increases your punching power."

- **Correct** and provide detailed feedback to the mixed martial artist when they are not performing the skill as intended. Corrective feedback entails giving the mixed martial artist feedback of where their performance is regarding a skillset goal and information on what they need to do to meet that goal. For example, "Johnny, you pivoted your back foot nicely when you threw the cross. Now remember to keep your left hand high to avoid being caught with a counter." Deliberate practice techniques should be incorporated to allow for mixed martial artists to improve a specific component of a skillset. For example, if a mixed martial artist keeps dropping their right hand when throwing the hook, cross, hook combo, the coach might require that the mixed martial artist throw the hook over and over again with focus on keeping the right hand up rather than repeating the entire combo.
- **Help** the mixed martial artist become fluent with a skill through fluency training and help them generalize the skills learned in the training environment through prescriptive or controlled sparring until these skills become a habit. An important approach is to help the mixed martial artist link their own behaviors to outcomes that will help them reach those goals.

Transferring Skills for Training to Combat

Remember, deliberate practice involves breaking down a specific skill, understating all its components, and accurately practicing each of those components over and over until a certain level of proficiency is achieved. This is only achieved through consistent reinforcement and corrective feedback of targeted skills while practice is progressively made more challenging over time. Too often, well-meaning coaches with a "sink or swim" mentality put a "green" mixed martial artist in the ring to spar or even compete without sufficient training and experience. It's a shame to think about how many potentially great mixed martial artists were literally beaten out of the sport because they were thrown into deep waters before they were even taught how to float.

This "sink or swim" mentality even applies to newly emerging skills being practiced by veteran mixed martial artists. Good coaches know that just throwing a mixed martial artist into the ring or cage without some level of proficiency will increase the likelihood that the mixed martial artist will fall back on old habits as the new skill has not been developed enough to be effective. As a result, the mixed martial artist may have less confidence and motivation to utilize a new or emerging skillset, or even less motivation to follow the coach's instruction as attempting the skillset may be extremely punishing (e.g., a mixed martial artist gets hurt or knocked out!).

> *Coaching is unlocking a person's potential to maximize their own performance. It is helping them to learn rather than teaching them.*
> --
> Timothy Gallwey

Thus, the coach's job is to increase the mixed martial artist's proficiency enough in the targeted skill so that they are more likely to perform it successfully during sparring and, ultimately, during the fight. This increases the likelihood that, when the mixed martial artist spars, the targeted skill will be met with reinforcement…in other words, the mixed martial artist will want to continue using the skill because it worked! Keep in mind, it's all about accurate deliberate practice. Practicing something incorrectly will only assist a mixed martial artist at becoming fluent at something potentially really bad.

DELIBERATE COACHING

As we've discussed, *deliberate practice* refers to practice that is purposeful and systematic. While regular practice might include mindless repetitions, deliberate practice requires focused attention and is conducted with the specific goal of improving performance. But it's not just enough to know precisely how to do something and build fluency under "safe" conditions. The mixed martial artist must also be able to perform this skill at the right time under live combat conditions. That is, the skill must occur automatically under a given combat condition, which usually includes a number of variables not present in typical training. An example of such a variable is the stress associated with the intensity of live combat or perhaps the anxiety a mixed martial arts athlete feels when performing in front of a live crowd. Borrowing from the familiar concept of deliberate practice, Gavoni and Weatherly (2019) described *deliberate coaching* as a behavioral coaching (Seniuk et al., 2013) approach that involves precise, purposeful, and systematic coaching interactions. In short, deliberate coaching supports the transference of skills developed through deliberate practice into live combat conditions. As an approach that's based on research on the science of behavior, deliberate coaching requires focused observation, the tracking of performance change, and feedback to shape socially valid, high-impact behavior. And when we say "socially valid," we mean behaviors that are acceptable to both the people implementing a particular coaching intervention (e.g., the MMA instructor) and those receiving the intervention (e.g., the MMA athlete). Let's take a look at the principles used to guide deliberate coaching (Gavoni & Weatherly, 2019):

Precise –

- Measurement of performance that is specific, detailed, and frequent. The mixed martial artist needs to be able to discriminate changes in and the outcomes of their behavior. If they cannot recognize the changes in or the outcomes of their own behavior, they are not likely to continue engaging in a specific skill.

- Clear distinction between the development of skills (training) and transference of skills. Hitting the bag, doing mitt work, and drilling arm bars from the guard are examples of skill development. Any form of simulated combat—such as live sparring, even light sparring—can be used to support the transference of a specific skill into combat conditions. The goal of the deliberate coach is to be precise in the skill being focused on.

- Feedback that is specific to a pinpointed skill or component of a skill.

- Feedback that links behavior to pinpointed results. Simply put, if the mixed martial artist does *this*, then *that* will happen.

Purposeful –

- Deliberately linked to actual combat-related outcomes. It's not just about helping the mixed martial artist perform better. It's about focusing on a very particular skill that will allow the mixed martial artist to achieve a very specific outcome.

- Intentionally designed with positive procedures. In other words, the coach is setting up conditions that increase the likelihood that the mixed martial artist will be successful, purposely focusing on what is good about the performance and then building from there until the skill is being performed in just the right way at just the right time under combat conditions. Just throwing the mixed martial artist in the cage to spar and hoping they will use a newly learned skill leaves much room for error and increases the likelihood that old habits will re-emerge.

- Sustained focus on a few pinpointed behaviors. If everything is important, nothing is important. While it may seem to slow the process down by focusing only a few components of a skill at a time, the research has shown this approach accelerates performance. So essentially, the deliberate coach goes slow to go fast!

Systematic –

- Uses specific behavioral procedures that have been experimentally demonstrated as effective and are repeatable. These are procedures like BST to develop the skills, engage in goal setting, pinpoint specific behaviors, and use a steady stream of feedback to shape or reinforce incremental improvement toward a desired outcome.

- Measures improvement against the mixed martial artist's own performance. The deliberate coach begins where the mixed martial artist is, and then systematically builds from there. Improvement is based on the mixed martial artist performing a skill a little bit better tomorrow than they did today.

> *You can only fight the way you practice.*
> --
> Miyomato Musashi

- Uses measurement of performance to guide coaching behavior. The measure of the deliberate coach is in the performance of the mixed martial artist. The deliberate coach avoids blaming. Rather, they use the progress visible in the mixed martial artist's performance, or lack thereof, to guide their coaching efforts.

- Uses social validity to monitor and guide coaching interventions. Specifically, the deliberate coach seeks feedback from those being coached to ensure both the skill being focused on and the coaching approaches are acceptable to the mixed martial artist.

The deliberate-coaching process is designed to work within any environment to improve performance, and this includes mixed martial arts. Each mixed martial arts gym has its own culture that needs to be acknowledged and respected, but in any gym, in any part of the world, *precision* allows for objectivity, *purposeful* coaching allows for sustained focus, and building performance under live combat conditions *systematically* ensures that skills are being shaped in measurable and manageable increments to achieve intended results.

Generalization

There are different training approaches, such as differentiated learning, that can help to ensure the mixed martial artist is engaging in deliberate practice. Differentiated learning, or differentiation, is linking what and how someone learns through the demonstration of proficiency, which in turn will determine the mixed martial artist's readiness for live combat. As we've discussed, deliberate practice and training is concerned with skill acquisition. That is, getting the mixed martial artist to do the right thing in the right way. Unfortunately, even becoming fluent in a technique doesn't ensure the mixed martial artist will be able to perform effectively under combat conditions. This reality has been a historical downfall of some of the more traditional martial arts as skills never have the chance to build fluency under live conditions. As a result, there are, unfortunately, many cases of a very skilled martial artist (e.g., a black belt) taking a beating from a far less skilled but more combat-seasoned opponent. To increase the likelihood that skills learned will transfer into fight conditions, training and coaching should be deliberate. Below is a guide for differentiation phases geared specifically toward shaping a mixed martial artist's proficiency for any given skill. Mixed martial artists will move through the phases below at different rates based on their overall experience and ability to learn.

1. New skillsets: When mixed martial artists are learning a new skillset, coaches should create structures that allow for safe deliberate practice. These structures include drills such as bag work, mitts, shadow boxing, or any no-contact drills that allow for high-repetition deliberate practice. During these training sessions, coaches should strive to provide high levels of feedback directly related to the specific skills.

2. Emerging skillsets: When mixed martial artists are demonstrating emerging skills in regard to a targeted skillset, coaches should create structures that involve low-impact, controlled sparring drills to allow for deliberate practice. For example, if a coach was teaching the slip-hook-cross combo, they might have two mixed martial artists spar lightly and only allow one of them to lead with the cross, while the other counters with the slip-hook-cross combo. This structure will allow the coach to observe and provide feedback under conditions that are closer to the fight condition. As the mixed martial artist moves closer to proficiency, the coach should allow the mixed martial artists to increase the intensity of sparring.

3. Proficiency with skillsets: When mixed martial artists have become proficient during controlled sparring drills, coaches should systematically begin permitting the mixed martial artist to add additional punches to the combo, with the goal being to finally allow the mixed martial artist to implement the skill during live sparring. During this phase, coaches should continue to observe and provide feedback, with the objective of fading prompts until the mixed martial artist can independently and fluently implement the skill. Remember, differentiation is a way for coaches to build deliberate practice routines for mixed martial artists based on their current needs, then progressively fade coaching as fluency increases to allow for generalization of skillsets into competition. These strategies also have the important effect of building a mixed martial artist's confidence.

Using Instructional Design

> *Practice does not make perfect.*
> *Only perfect practice makes perfect.*
> --
> Vince Lombardi

For those of you interested in precisely, purposely, and systematically building out your own deliberate practice and deliberate coaching sessions to accelerate learning, skill acquisition, and performance, we have provided essential guiding questions related to achieving targeted performance objectives. This approach is rooted in instructional design and promotes shifting the control from the mixed martial arts instructor to the student so that they can effectively perform the right skill at the right time in the right way, outside the training environment (Vargas & Fraley, 1984):

Primary Objective (What is the intended outcome?)
1. Knowledge – What information will mixed martial artists need to be able to recall to meet this objective?
    a. How will this be measured?
2. Performance – What skills will mixed martial artists need to be able to perform to meet this objective?

    a. Skill 1
        i. How will the skill be instructed?
        ii. How will the skill be modeled?
        iii. How will the mixed martial artist have an opportunity to rehearse the skill?
        iv. How will the mixed martial artist receive regular feedback related to the skill?
        v. How will skill acquisition be measured?

    b. Skill 2
        i. How will the skill be instructed?
        ii. How will the skill be modeled?
        iii. How will the mixed martial artist have an opportunity to rehearse the skill?
        iv. How will the mixed martial artist receive regular feedback related to the skill?
        v. How will skill acquisition be measured?

- c. Skill 3
    - i. How will the skill be instructed?
    - ii. How will the skill be modeled?
    - iii. How will the mixed martial artist have an opportunity to rehearse the skill?
    - iv. How will the mixed martial artist receive regular feedback related to the skill?*
    - v. How will skill acquisition be measured?
3. Simulation – How will opportunities be created for mixed martial artists to practice the skill under conditions that closely mirror actual combat conditions?
4. Evaluation
    - a. How will competence be measured?
    - b. How will social validity be measured?
        - i. In regard to instruction?
        - ii. In regard to knowledge/skills learned?

USING DATA TO ACCELERATE PERFORMANCE

Professional combat athletes, while widely respected in and outside the sports field, too often find themselves capitalizing on the absolute bare minimum of training equipment and technology. If you walk into the training facilities of most major sports, you'd likely be impressed by the sport-specific (and even position-specific) equipment and measures available to the athletes. With the exception of a few of the elite gyms around the globe, most MMA gyms typically only have mats on the floor (and wall if the athlete is "lucky"), a few bags hanging off the wall, and a bench with a small assortment of dumbbells.

> *Errors using inadequate data are much less than those using no data at all.*
>
> --
>
> Charles Babbage

If professional combat sports were music, it might be considered the Blues of the sports world given the stark contrast between the training practices and resources of other sport disciplines. The good news is that following the behavioral scientific principles outlined in this book will allow mixed martial artists to enhance their performance regardless of their training facility. In fact, the science of human behavior might be considered the Blues of psychology or performance fields given the economy and, thankfully, simplistic nature of the practices. Understanding and applying some of the basic concepts learned up to this point, and those you will learn in following sections, will allow any mixed martial artist and coach, regardless of the availability of equipment, to improve performance beyond the martial artist's current state.

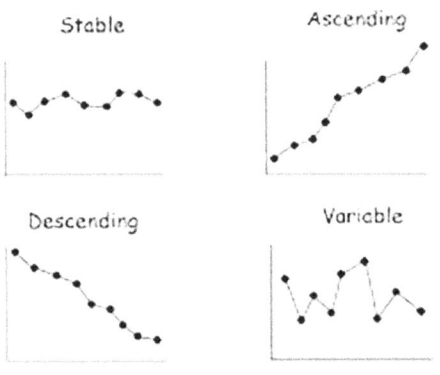

Table 4. Data Graphs.

Simply put, sport is behavior, and the technology of the science of human behavior, or applied behavior analysis (ABA), can (and should!) be used to improve athletic performance. As a science, ABA relies on data as illustrated in Table 4 above, to improve the behavior being focused on. In the case of MMA, data might be used to prepare for a fight, strengthen skills, or improve tactics during training sessions. Incidentally, data for many in martial arts may seem like an uncomfortable term reserved for folks working in the world of computers and software. But it doesn't have to be a four-letter word! When used to help mixed martial artists improve performance and outcomes, data becomes indispensable.

Data exists in many forms. For example, data can be text or numbers written on paper, facts amassed in somebody's mind, or (as commonly perceived) bits and bytes stored in a computer. Data in the wide world of sports has become a standard practice in many disciplines. In fact, teams and athletes are now able to capture large chunks of data through a variety of sophisticated technologies used to gather common measurements like body composition and uncommon measurements like eye gaze. Though these processes may be time-consuming and even costly (they don't have to be, though), the return on investment is often measured in large fight purses. While combat sports like boxing and MMA typically utilize common sources of data, there is a huge opportunity for growth with little to no financial investment.

In MMA, evaluating a variety of sources of data can allow mixed martial artists and MMA teams to monitor and adjust fighters' training regimens to produce better outcomes. There are often two sources of data used in training: leading indicators and lagging indicators. *Leading indicators* are the data that match up with our day-to-day activities—for example, body weight, miles ran, and rounds sparred. *Lagging indicators* are the data we collect "after the fact" or are more historical in nature—for example, W-L record, decision type (KO, submission), and success against fight styles.

As MMA continues to evolve, the availability of a variety of data sources provides mixed martial artists and camps the ability to efficiently and effectively shape a fighter's performance. With fight purses and endorsements growing exponentially, mixed martial artists and training camps can increase their odds of an even higher purse by capitalizing on existing data sources and utilizing some simple processes standard to ABA. In the next chapter, we will provide you with a very powerful yet simple data collection process that can be used to improve performance and celebrate successful achievement of belt ranking.

USING THE PERFORMANCE EVALUATION SHEET

TRADITIONALLY, TO achieve a belt, students attend belt testing ceremonies where students are awarded a belt ranking based on the instructor's subjective evaluation of students' performance of targeted skills. Unfortunately, because of the subjectivity of the process, MMA students who fail to achieve a belt rank following testing can walk away frustrated as they are unsure of where they went wrong. This often occurs because they do not have data that specifies precisely what they did well and what components of a skill or skills they need to improve upon. Think about it. If a student was required to perform 20 different techniques composed of 5–10 different components, there are potentially hundreds of errors a student might make. Fortunately, MMA Science solves this problem through a precise data collection process captured through Performance Evaluation Sheets, as in the example below.

Performance Evaluation Sheet		
Jab		
Target	**Yes**	**No**
1. Stance		
2. Advancing Step Front Foot		
3. Strike		
4. Advancing Step Back Foot		
5. Feet Spacing		
6. Retreating Back Foot		
7. Retreating Step Front Foot		
8. Feet Spacing		
9. Stance		
Percentage Correct	_____%	

Table 5. Performance Evaluation Sheet.

Performance Evaluation Sheets are provided to make data collection simple for the coach. In addition, they can be used by students to self-coach and self-evaluate prior to actual belt testing. Each skill has a scoresheet, as seen below in the example for the jab. The scoresheet is designed to capture whether the student correctly demonstrated each component of a targeted skill. For example, the jab has nine components – starting with the MMA stance, followed by foot work, striking, and the return to the MMA stance. As each component is demonstrated by the student, the coach checks a "yes" or "no" to indicate whether the component was performed correctly. When using the evaluation sheets for belt testing, we suggest taking the following five steps:

1. Choose the skill to evaluate and have the task analysis (see below example of the jab) readily available for the coach to use in evaluating and marking "yes" versus "no" on the evaluation sheet.

Jab	
Description: The jab is a *pivotal technique* central to many areas related to offensive and defensive techniques. Pivotal techniques provide opportunities for improvement in other techniques and associated desired outcomes.	
1. Stance	All elements of MMA stance in place
2. Advancing Step Front Foot	Push off the ball of the rear foot, lift the lead foot, and take half step forward
3. Strike	Propel lead hand from MMA stance ballistically forward with rear hand held at temple
4. Advancing Step Back Foot	Rear foot follows and moves equal distance forward
5. Feet Spacing	Feet return to original foot spacing
6. Retreating Back Foot	Push off the ball of the lead foot, lift the rear foot, and take half step backward
7. Retreating Step Front Foot	Lead foot follows and moves equal distance backward
8. Feet Spacing	Feet return to original foot spacing
10. Stance	Return to MMA stance
Pictures	

Table 6. Scoresheet for Jab.

2. Check-off yes or no to indicate whether the component was performed correctly. If the student misses only a component or two during the first attempt, we recommend the coach model the skill and then provide them another opportunity to demonstrate it. Sometimes testing conditions can have a negative impact on performance, so providing the student a second opportunity can be helpful. If the student does not meet the criteria during the second attempt, the coach should move on to the next skill, and the prior particular skill is scored as a fail.

3. Continue evaluating each skill until all skills have all been scored.

Below is an example of a completed evaluation sheet for the jab. Note that eight of the nine components were scored "Yes" because they were performed correctly, and one component was scored a "No" because it was performed incorrectly. This resulted in a score of 88%, which is simply the result of dividing 8 by 9. Please note that different skills have a different number of components, which will impact the percentages. For example, where missing one component of the jab resulted in a score of 88% because there was a total of nine components, a skill with five components and one missing component would be scored at 80%. In some cases, missing a component or element of a component wouldn't compromise the skill (e.g., the MMA stance is slightly wide). For other skills missing a certain component would render the skill completely ineffective (e.g., failing to point the thumb up on an armbar). Accordingly, the coach will need to determine the passing criteria for each skill.

Jab		
Target	**Yes**	**No**
1. Stance	Y	
2. Advancing Step Front Foot	Y	
3. Strike	Y	
4. Advancing Step Back Foot	Y	
5. Feet Spacing	Y	
6. Retreating Back Foot		N
7. Retreating Step Front Foot	Y	
8. Feet Spacing	Y	
9. Stance	Y	
Percentage Correct	88%	

Table 7. Completed Evaluation Sheet for Jab.

4. Complete the Total Performance Score Sheet, and divide the total number of skills scored "Yes" by the total number of scores. Make any notations if needed that should be reviewed with the student. In the example below, the student passed 24 out of 30 skills, which resulted in a score of 80%. Note that, in the example, we have set the passing criteria at 80%; however, we recommend the criteria progressively increase with each belt rank.

5. When appropriate, review the scores with the student so that they know exactly what they did well and exactly where they need to work. In some cases, when certain criteria are met (e.g., 60%–79% in the example below), coaches may wish to provide the student another opportunity to retest on another day as opposed to having to wait until the next regularly scheduled belt ranking test.

USING THE PERFORMANCE EVALUATION SHEET

	Skills Passed	Yes	No	Notes
	Total Performance Scorecard (Example)			
Striking	MMA Stance	Y		
	Jab	Y		Good snap on jab
	Cross	Y		
	Straight Knee		N	Failed to frame and return to MMA stance
	Rear Leg Push kick		N	Failed to frame and take step the lead foot out
	Lead Leg Push kick	Y		
	Basic Head Movement		N	Failed to maintain correct posture
	Linear Foot Work	Y		
	Lateral Foot Work	Y		
	Parry Jab	Y		
	Block Cross	Y		
	Block Straight Knee	Y		
	Block Rear Leg Push Kick	Y		
	Block Lead Leg Push Kick	Y		
Grappling	Underhook	Y		
	Overhook		N	Failed to fully overhook the arm
	Pummeling	Y		
	Double Underhook	Y		
	Body Lock	Y		
	Collar Tie	Y		
	Full Guard Top	Y		
	Basic Double leg	Y		Good posture and penetration step
	Side Control Top	Y		
	Basic Bridging		N	Failed to elevate hips
	Bridge and Reach	Y		
	Bridge and Roll		N	Failed to elevate hips and complete roll
	Bridge and Shrimp	Y		
	Full Guard Bottom	Y		
	Side Control Bottom	Y		Tight side control; good knee positioning
	Tech MMA Get Up	Y		
	Total	80%		**Scoring Criteria:** 80%> = Pass 79%–60% = Eligible for Retest >59% = Fail

Table 8. Total Performance Scorecard.

While we've discussed the use of the score sheets in the context of a coach scoring for the purpose of belt ranking, please know that the process can also be used by the MMA student attempting to assess and improve their own performance *prior* to actual belt rankings. To do this, the student simply needs to have a peer observe and score them using the provided task analysis and scorecards. In fact, this data can easily be popped into a graph and used to monitor improvement as belt testing nears!

STYLES MAKE FIGHTS

With almost a quarter century of fighting and coaching, we have had the fortune to collaborate and train with many world-class mixed martial artists, champions, and UFC vets. Moreover, we've been exposed to the teachings of master coaches. During this time, we've observed or have been the recipient of a variety of philosophies and approaches to the combat sports. Oddly enough, some approaches have been radically conflicting. For example, champion boxing trainer Milton Lacroix teaches mixed martial artists to fight off the ball of their back foot with the lead hand held below the waist. This approach directly conflicts with Angelo Dundee suggesting that the mixed martial artist's rear foot should remain more flatfooted with the guard held high (which is odd considering he trained Muhammad Ali, who had a style similar to what Milton taught). Similarly, world champion Muay Thai coaches compel their students to deliberately plod forward, while Olympic boxing coaches urge their students to use lateral movement to create angles off their opponent's aggression. The same goes for the grappling world: champion BJJ coaches recommend one nuanced approach to a takedown, but champion wrestling coaches recommend another.

"They can't all be right," we used to contemplate. But given their success, they couldn't all be wrong, either, could they? Well, the answer, from our perspective, is they were all right…just not all of the time. Clear as mud? How could they be right sometimes? The solution, as you will see, can be found in fighting styles!

Styles Defined

As the old saying goes, styles make fights. But what are styles, and how is it they "make" fights? What if Mike Tyson had devoted his training toward a style like Muhammad Ali's? Or conversely, if Ali attempted to use the "peek-a-boo" style mastered by Tyson? Can you imagine what Tyson—with his short, stocky build—would like as he "floats like a butterfly, stings like a bee"? Or Ali—with his height and long reach—attempting to slip inside to explode with massive hooks. The thought, for some, might actually be humorous. Would each boxer have become a reigning champion? It doesn't take an expert analyst to figure this one out!

Elements of styles are essentially observable behaviors. Styles can be considered a combination of high-frequency behaviors that mixed martial artists apply under specific combat conditions.

> *Absorb what is useful, discard what is useless,*
> *and add what is specifically your own.*
> --
> Bruce Lee

More specifically, styles are made up of a complex interplay between genetics, physiological characteristics, historical factors, and contact with environmental factors (Gavoni & Gomez, 2014). We contend that those involved in combat sports would benefit by having a deeper understanding of styles. "One style fits all" philosophies limit potential. Consideration of characteristics such height and reach to "fit" mixed martial artists with the most effective style will accelerate performance.

Styles Happen

Coaching has a lot to do with the core skillsets that make up styles. However, many styles develop in the absence of deliberate coaching, or even contrary to a coach's specific instruction. Why? Styles often develop inadvertently. When sparring, mixed martial artists come in contact with naturally occurring reinforcers (i.e., it's working) and punishers (i.e., it isn't working). For example, something tells us that coaches did not tell Ali, "Keep your hands down!" In fact, if you listen closely to Angelo Dundee in Ali's early fights, you can hear exactly the opposite. "Keep your hands up," Dundee fervently urges as Ali effortlessly dances around his opponents firing lightning-fast jabs.

We contend that, early in Ali's training history, he likely came into contact with reinforcement (i.e., success) very quickly by using a low-hanging, relaxed jab that allowed him to take advantage of his incredible reach. Not only did Ali land more jabs, but he likely received less punishment than his opponents who used a high guard. You see, Ali's style employed the hidden defense of distance and angles to capitalize on his reach. He didn't need to keep his hands up—when he used this style, his opponents literally couldn't reach him!

Styles Evolve

Like in Darwin's theory of evolution, only the strongest skills "survive" as they increase the mixed martial artist's ability to compete. In the case of combat sports, the skills attempted by the mixed martial artist that prove most effective are the ones naturally selected. These skills will likely endure and evolve to become part of the mixed martial artist's lasting repertoire. Like the novice mixed martial artist who compromises countering ability as he leans away from a punch, certain techniques aren't sustainable. However, because these skills might be garnering the mixed martial artist an immediate return on investment, they are likely to continue.

The good news is that quality coaching or sparring that provides natural consequences tend to shape performance. In Ali's case, behaviors that were "naturally selected" were lateral foot movement alongside a low-hanging, long-distance jab. These skills proved superior to even the most dangerous opponents, so Ali continued to use them. A shorter boxer like Joe Frazier, for instance, would never have obtained the coveted world heavyweight title using this approach. Frazier needed head movement and shorter hooking punches to be effective.

Styles Strategically Applied

What we can see from this illustration is that certain things work for some mixed martial artists much better than others, especially when fighting particular opponents. It's not uncommon to hear mixed martial artists say things like "I hate sparring tall guys" or "those short, compact mixed martial artists give me a hard time." One could argue that these same mixed martial artists might learn to love sparring these same opponents. Specifically, this might be the case if the mixed martial artists were able to successfully develop a competitive strategy that falls within the parameters of the style for which they're best suited. In other words, by considering the style of the mixed martial artist relative to their opponent, coaches may be able to more effectively build a strategic plan to capitalize on strengths and accelerate the acquisition of skills that fall within the mixed martial artist's physical propensities. An example of this approach is training Tyson in the "peek-a-boo" style to turn his height and reach "disadvantage" into a competitive edge.

Styles Classified

For analyzing styles, we propose a classification system made up of three styles: short-range, mid-range, and long-range styles. To illustrate, let's look at champions in boxing and MMA as a model of the proposed style classifications:

Short-range style:
- Boxing: Mike Tyson, Joe Frazier
- MMA: Johnny Hendricks, Quinton Jackson

Mid-range style:
- Boxing: Julio César Chávez, Felix Trinidad
- MMA: Donald Cerrone, BJ Penn

Long-range style:
- Boxing: Vladimir Klitchko, Tommy Hearns
- MMA: Anderson Silva, Lyoto Machida

Mixed martial artists do not typically fight using a style that fits cleanly into one specific class. Instead, they tend to transition fluidly through elements of each style within a fight as conditions require. However, we suggest fluent practitioners of a specific style, as illustrated by the classification system above, likely follow the 80–20 rule: 80% of the time they use their "go-to stylistic skills," and 20% of the time they utilize elements that fall within the other two classifications. This is not to suggest that all mixed martial artists use an 80/20 mix, or the same mixed martial artists use the same ratio for each fight. For instance, one mixed martial artist might be utilizing long-range striking 60% of the time, mid-range striking 20% of the time, and short-range striking 10% of the time.

The same mixed martial artist who understands styles and is aware of an opponent's significant reach advantage or grappling disadvantage might adapt their game as follows: 10% long-range, 40% mid-range, and 60% short-range striking. We would suggest that the closer a mixed martial artist comes to applying a specific style 100% of the time, the closer they come to the purest form of the style classification.

> *Real style is never right or wrong,*
> *it's a matter of being yourself on purpose.*
>
> --
>
> G. Bruce Boyer

Styles Make Fights

Styles do make fights. If Ali were to fight his doppelganger, there would likely be lots of dancing and very little fighting. Fortunately, most of Ali's opponents moved forward. The result? "Good style match-ups" and exciting fights. For mixed martial artists, style adjustments to the style of their opponents can be the difference between winning and losing. Thus, understanding styles is critical for developing a mixed martial artist's skillset and for strategic fight planning. Can you imagine Tyson training and fighting like Ali, or vice versa? It's safe to say they would have not reached the pinnacle of the sport had they not perfected a style that matched genetic predispositions like height and reach.

While the above illustrates the classification of striking styles, the same concept is easily applied to the grappling side of MMA. We've all heard certain mixed martial artists described as "grinders" as an example of a certain "style" applied by some mixed martial artists. We leave it up to you, the reader, to observe and begin looking for the dynamic "styles" of different mixed martial artists and then comparing their body styles and approaches to your own evolving styles. Sometimes these comparisons can provide you with a road map for developing certain aspects of your own style.

THE PSYCHOLOGY OF THE FIGHTER

The difference between MMA and other combat sports such as boxing or wrestling is that there are many, *many* paths to victory, or defeat. This aspect is essentially a result of the vast array of skills and skillsets practiced by MMA artists. Practicing various skillsets and becoming better at each skill never ensures a victory; rather, it increases the likelihood or probability of a win. To ignore the mental or psychological facet of the game certainly increases the probability of a path to defeat. Joe Rogan once stated, "During that walk to the octagon…fights are won and lost in the mind of the fighter…" We agree with the statement, but the psychology of a fighter does not start and end with the walk—it's about how the mind of the fighter is prepped and conditioned during training camp. Assuming that the physical training takes care of the mental component is a faulty assumption…a trap. Therefore, the million-dollar question is this: "What elements contribute to a 'good' training camp?" In general, everyone would agree that quality coaches, quality diet, quality physical training, quality rehab, and quality mental training make up a good training camp. All these elements are closely linked and directly affect one another. A fighter cannot expect to have the best coaches in the world but skimp on the diet and expect to have great results, for example. The quality of the fighter's diet regimen will also affect the quality of training, the time it takes to recover, and ultimately, the fighter's mental status as the performance during training quickly transfers into the fighter's psyche. The goal of camp is to have all of these elements aligned at the highest level. Thus, in this section, we focus on the mental or psychological component.

Similar to the vast array of submission options taught in BJJ, there are many aspects to the psychological approach to conditioning the athlete's mind. We focus on one of the most critical—a fighter's confidence—and then we move to the premise of the optimal zone of functioning. We must point out that all psychological components interact at some level and don't exist in isolation. For example, a fighter's confidence plays a large role in determining whether a fighter can enter their zone in camp or in competition. It is a false conception that many coaches and athletes hold that the only way to build confidence is to accrue wins and practice longer and harder. Though this is in part true, it is an oversimplified belief and often prohibits mixed martial artists and coaches from fully engaging and using all the known confidence-building strategies proven by research to enhance confidence in performers. Importantly, confidence is a state of mind. One cannot touch confidence or even see it, but one can observe its impact on a fighter's behavior and how they perform. However, there are known psychological tactics that must be used to improve an athlete's belief in their own abilities—tactics that go above and beyond physical training and competing. As we mentioned previously, executing a fight plan can be impacted by many factors, such as diet or rehab, but the overarching aura of high confidence is exactly what a fighter wants to feel. So how does one reach that point?

> *Fear is the greatest obstacle to learning.*
> *But fear is your best friend. Fear is like fire.*
> *If you learn to control it, you let it work for you.*
> *If you don't learn to control it,*
> *it will destroy you and everything around you.*
>
> --
>
> Cus D'Amato

Confidence is one of the most important psychological states in determining performance quality in sports and is one of the best predictors of performance. In other words, the more confident the athlete, the better they are likely to perform. And yes, good physical training, a good diet, and good rehab can enhance confidence, but there is more. For research purposes, we typically refer to confidence as self-efficacy. The terms *confidence* and *self-efficacy* are basically interchangeable; however, self-efficacy is more specific than confidence, and self-efficacy details the athlete's perceived capability to accomplish a specific feat. For example, an MMA fighter may have high self-efficacy in their ability to execute a takedown, but a lower sense of efficacy in their standup. Through this example, one can see that, speaking only in terms of confidence, the meaningful differences between being confident in one skill yet not feeling confident in another can be lost. It's important, then, not only to determine a fighter's perceived efficacy but also to tune a training camp based on this premise.

Therefore, considering that self-efficacy is task-specific, we cannot say an MMA fighter is either confident or not confident. Speaking in these terms is an example of using a machete to perform surgery. The fighter may feel more confident in their standup mid-range game, but less confident in a short-range game, or perhaps the fighter has good confidence in their takedown defense, but less confidence fighting out of the guard. Keep in mind that, for a coach and fighter, it is important to be aware of all the confidence-performance combinations perceived by an MMA fighter. Coaches sometimes verbalize this as strengths and weaknesses, which is okay, too. But it's a perception the fighter maintains, and that's why it must be addressed first from a psychological standpoint. If it is not approached this way, then coaches and mixed martial artists find themselves overestimating or misjudging their overall confidence prior to a fight. A fighter and their coach should take stock in all the skills the fighter is required to have, then attempt to grade the quality of those specific skillsets, such as the guard, submissions, ability on top, on the bottom, takedown defense, head movement, and so on.

Next, those skills should be graded in comparison to an upcoming opponent, for example. Depending on the opponent, wrestling may be an advantage in one fight, but may not be in the next fight. This is why it's often important to capitalize on a fighter's strengths and fortify the fighter's weaknesses *specific* to a given strategy or opponent. The goal of camp should *not* be to help the fighter become well-rounded. Instead, the goal should be to make the camp "fighter-centric" by tailoring the camp to developing or enhancing specific skills to strengthen the fighter's confidence for a specific fight. This approach will equate to a higher probability of winning.

> *To see a man beaten not by a better opponent*
> *but by himself is a tragedy.*
>
> --
>
> Cus D'Amato

Self-Efficacy

How can a fighter strengthen their confidence? First, we will refer to confidence as self-efficacy from this point forward. To start, a big key is to stay away from determining overall self-efficacy, as we stated above—instead, perceptions of self-efficacy should be broken down into components. Once broken down into its components, the *sources* of self-efficacy can be applied to each aspect. Sources are the determinants that influence or affect self-efficacy. There are generally four major sources (Bandura, 1997): mastery experiences (prior performance), verbal persuasion (coaching advice), vicarious experience (watching another fighter accomplish what you think you can), and emotional/physiological states (the state of mind and body).

The best way to discuss these sources is to exemplify each source with an aspect of the fight game and then apply each source to the context. Let's say, for example, our fighter typically uses a long-range striking style in their standup. Below is a chart of how this specific skill might be broken down into its components. Once the skill is broken down and graded, sources of efficacy can be applied to each component to ultimately improve the fighter's overall sense of self-efficacy related to this skill. Take notice that our fighter in this example grades high in offense but low in defense. Therefore, the fighter needs to enhance their defense, build confidence in this area, and thus avoid having a false sense of efficacy in their overall ability.

Long-Range Striking	Coach's Grade (1–10)	Keys to Success
Stance	8	As compared to the "squared stance" (i.e., feet around 10 a.m. and 4 p.m. for the orthodox fighter) required for the short-range styles (e.g., Mike Tyson), the fighter's stance is more linear in nature (e.g., feet around 11 a.m. and 5 p.m. for the orthodox fighter)
Head Movement	8	Where short-range mixed martial artists are often best served with increased head movement characterized by "slipping" or "rolling," long-range striking styles tend to be more effective with "micro head movement." That is, head movement that is "just enough" to remain out of range of the opponent, but close enough to engage in offense when provided the opportunity.

Foot Movement	7	"Micro foot work" (i.e., shuffling, short steps) applied with this style is typically most effective as it constantly allows the long-range fighter to remain in a position to throw punches, whether moving forward, backward, or laterally. With this footwork, mixed martial artists can "stop on a dime," if you will, as opposed to mixed martial artists who use more plodding footwork, or footwork that engages in lengthier steps.
Offense	8	Long-range fighting offense might be thought of as the "sniper" of the striking arts. Because of the hand speed and countering nature of this style, combos are intended to be thrown very long, which increases the focus on straight punches. A lowered guard with relaxed shoulders guard allow for relaxed and swift strikes. Punches are thrown with hand speed, accuracy, and relatively minimal trunk rotation. Short range styles mixed martial artists tend to throw higher rates of power punches that require more trunk rotation. With a long-range style, the fighter more often picks their power punches and therefore only engages in full trunk rotation at the perceived opportune moment.
Defense	5	By fighting long and using micro footwork coupled with lateral movement, defense is simultaneously incorporated as the fighter strives to remain just outside the opponent's reach. Distance with a relaxed, lower-than-usual guard is often a key to defense with this style as the fighter can remain just outside of their opponent's reach. Where the hand positioning for short- or mid-range mixed martial artists tends to remain close or even tightly fitted to the head, long-range mixed martial artists are often effective by placing their hands out in front of their bodies. While mixed martial artists who move forward are typically best served applying a higher guard, long-range mixed martial artists are able to parry or catch punches on their arms prior to contact with the head or torso.
Counter Striking	6	One of the strengths of this style is that it can be used to draw (bait) the opponent into a well-timed counter attack as the opponent has the illusion the fighter can be attacked because of their lowered guard. In other words, opponents perceive an opening that is not actually there, thus increasing the opportunity for a counter attack. Some have even called it a "bait and switch" technique. Here, fighters utilize their footwork and distance to avoid an opponent's offense and then capitalize with a well-timed counter strike.

Table 9. On how a specific skill might be broken down into its components.

Once each component of the skill is unpacked and graded, and there is a physical path to improvement outlined, then the psychological piece related to self-efficacy should be initiated, as detailed in the table below.

Sources of Self-Efficacy	Keys to Improvement
Mastery Experience	*Mental* – The fighter is to reacquaint themselves with prior-fighting success using this style. This includes visualization techniques and film study. *Physical* – The fighter must engage in exchanges with the coach and then in sparring, accumulating gradual successes with each encounter.
Verbal Persuasion	*Mental* – The fighter's coach must regularly provide meaningful feedback and reinforcement letting the fighter know they are progressing on the right track.
Vicarious Experience	*Mental* – The fighter must be in position to watch other mixed martial artists achieve success with the long-range style, ensuring the fighter understands they too can execute with success. The fighter can accomplish this through both direct observation and film study.
Emotional/Physiological States	*Mental* – The fighter must study their own emotions related to their best and worst performances of the past, and understand what mindset gives them the best chance to perform optimally. *Physical* – The fighter should train under conditions that best mimic real-fight conditions, giving the fighter a chance to experience the heightened emotional states and how they relate to performance. This includes breathing exercises and heart-rate control strategies.

Table 10. On the physical path to improvement, then the psychological piece related to self-efficacy.

This is a rough example of how a fighter and their coach can start to build self-efficacy by breaking down the components of one specific skill and applying all the sources of efficacy to *each* component of long-range striking. On average, our fighter in this example grades high in long-range striking, but there are key areas where they are relatively weak—specifically, in counter striking and defense. Therefore, without this systematic analysis, the fighter is more likely to enter a fight with an overestimated sense of self-efficacy in their long-range style. The point here is to exemplify the complexity of a specific skillset and the self-efficacy related to the skill to avoid the tendency of some coaches and mixed martial artists to misjudge confidence. Coaches and mixed martial artists can use the various sources of efficacy to improve overall confidence and understand that enhancing performance is far more than just training longer and harder. Instead, the goal is to become more confident by developing each skill through quality practice, *not* focusing on an overall sense of confidence. This means focusing on the process and applying each source of efficacy, not focusing on the outcome. The outcome will take care of itself.

The next component of the mental game we will discuss is the concept of the optimal zone of functioning. One cannot focus on the zone until the premise of self-efficacy is established. The optimal zone revolves around the principle of psychological and physical stress. Psychological stress can be perceived as fear, whereas physical stress can be seen as muscle fatigue, for example. However, in sport science, we classify stress as optimal or not optimal, and this operates on a continuum. In other words, stress in training can have positive results on performance, but only up to a certain point; too much stress results in decreased performance. And we're not just referring to overtraining or overtraining syndrome. If an athlete is overly stressed due to excessive weight loss, for example, the physiological stress can lead to decreased performance during training, which of course ties into the mental status (reduced confidence). As we just discussed, confidence, or self-efficacy, is one of the greatest predictors of performance. Thus, what we see here is the interaction between physiological states of the body and psychological states of the mind.

We understand that there is a negative relationship between excessive stress during training and a fighter's confidence. In other words, as the fighter consistently exceeds their optimal states of stress throughout training, the quality of their training decreases, thus negatively affecting their confidence. A reduction in confidence equals a reduced probability of winning. There are scientific techniques to gauge the amount of stress and determine its effect on performance. There are also good coaches who can intuitively detect when a fighter is beyond their optimal levels of stress during training.

Individual Zone of Optimal Functioning

The individual zone of optimal functioning (IZOF), generally speaking, is about performing optimally based on the fighter's individual capabilities. The zone can be delineated through the level of stress or activation a fighter exhibits while performing. The zone is not just a construct that should be the focus in relation to the actual fight-night performance. Rather, the zone should be identified and widely apparent during training camp routines in order to engage in deliberate practice. A fighter who is overly stressed or exhausted from excessive weight-loss strategies, or even the persistent thought of it, will likely be prevented from entering their IZOF, period. The zone is expansive and can be defined by the fighter's emotional states, physiological states, or cognitive states (Edmonds et al., 2012). A good coach can intuitively understand these categories and intervene when necessary. That is, a good coach creates practice routines that simulate the intensity of a real fight where the fighter engages in the exercise while becoming comfortable with and aware of what their IZOF. A good sport scientist would know how to gauge these states and demonstrate how, for example, excessively high heart-rate patterns or poor heart-rate recovery, or reports of poor mood states, are related to poor performance while training. All of these aspects will determine whether the fighter is practicing in their IZOF. Are heart-rate parameters being properly monitored during camp? Are mood states and levels of efficacy being gauged? If not, then it's likely the fighter is being exposed to excessive stress, and the subsequent poor mood states will reduce the likelihood of entering the IZOF during training, negating deliberate practice and negatively impacting confidence. If the fighter perceives negative physiological or emotional states, then this will also lower their confidence. A fighter who is excessively stressed mentally and physically from excessive weight-loss or physically training too hard with little recovery will likely be training outside a targeted heart-rate zone and may burn out quicker during practice and require longer periods of recovery to lower their heart rate before re-engaging in the next routine.

Athletes can find their IZOFs as a result of being aware of the associated emotional and physiological states of their performance. In other words, an MMA fighter may perform optimally when they are angry and scared at the same time with a minimal level of arousal (laymen's term is nervousness). This state would equate to performing optimally or being in the optimal zone of functioning. Though it doesn't guarantee a win, being in this zone gives the fighter the highest probability to perform optimally and perhaps win. Notably, optimal zones shouldn't be confused with flow states as flow states don't have to be associated with performance-based scenarios.

The critical piece to determining and finding the zone is using measurement tools. Subjective data, such as mood states or emotional states, can often be used in reference to finding zones, though we prefer using objective data in conjunction with subjective accounts. Many measurement tools are available on the market today, which allows for the collection of a variety data to be collected in real time or during performance scenarios. Such tools are capable of collecting data such as the speed of movement, heart-rate parameters, and breathing rate. These metrics can be important as heart rate, breathing, and movement are very valuable data points when defining a fighter's IZOF. We've been able to determine a fighter's IZOF by gauging heart-rate zones during striking combo executions, the time it took to recover and re-enter that zone during another attack, and then the optimal breathing patterns to mediate the fighter's heart-rate zones during simulated attacks and "breaks" between attacks. Between rounds, it was used as a means of "relaxing" the fighter through specific and guided breathing techniques before re-engaging. Optimal zones are all gauged by comparing each zone (physiological or psychological) and correlating it with the quality of performance.

Helping fighters find their IZOF can be an extremely powerful approach for accelerating performance; however, there is still another component to consider when helping the mixed martial artist reach their maximum potential. Overcoming fear and anxiety.

OVERCOMING FEAR AND ANXIETY

The stress experienced by fighters may trump that experienced by athletes in any other professional sport globally. Concerns about performing well in front of a crowd under the added pressure of an opponent attempting to inflict bodily harm creates great pressure that progressively increases and peaks up to the moment before the bell rings. While some stress has been found to optimize performance, too much stress has adverse effects.

Fear and anxiety are often recognized by mixed martial artists as the largest and most difficult challenges to navigate. Too much of either can result in a self-fulfilling prophecy as the very things the fighter feared come to fruition as the result of a performance-killing "adrenaline dump" in the early moments of a fight.

Common approaches to managing fear include ignoring or suppressing it, but how effective are these approaches? And what if they actually hurt as opposed to help mixed martial artists? Suppressing fear and anxiety has been compared to holding a ball underwater (Polk et al., 2016). The effort becomes unsustainable, and as soon as the ball is let go, it jettisons to the surface. The larger the ball (i.e., the larger the anxiety), the harder it becomes to maintain, and the bigger the explosion into the air once it's released. In the case of fear and anxiety, this "explosion" is often analogous to the aforementioned adrenaline dump.

> *I do what is mine to do;*
> *the rest does not disturb me.*
> --
> Marcus Aurelius

Often times, fear is simply a "boogie man" drummed up by what might be considered an overactive imagination. In other words, we assign value to things and then become "hooked" (more on this later) on our self-defeating thoughts. For many mixed martial artists, these thoughts are often related to the fear of losing, fear of letting people down, fear of being embarrassed, or fear of not performing well in front of fans and loved ones. When these thoughts rise to the surface, it is not uncommon for mixed martial artists to be told "don't think about it." But the problem is, mixed martial artists then get hooked on thinking about not thinking about it. This thinking wastes precious energy, has little return on investment, and is even counterproductive, as noted above regarding the "suppression" technique. If only the mixed martial artist could simply "do what it is his to do" (e.g., train hard, eat right, listen to coaches, perform well, etc.) and not be disturbed by fear and anxiety. Well, it turns out that Aurelius was really on to something. A growing body of research behind acceptance commitment therapy (ACT) suggests that the key to overcoming fear, anxiety, and the unproductive behaviors that come from those feeling is to simply "do what is yours to do." In other words, accepting some thoughts and feelings that have shown up and then focusing on behaviors that lead toward what one values has two amazing effects: (a) it accelerates one's performance toward goals, and (b) it simultaneously reduces unhealthy rumination that often leads to self-defeating thoughts and behaviors that move one away from their values. Fortunately, there is a practical tool known as the ACT matrix that can be used by mixed martial artists and coaches to help mitigate fear and anxiety while strategically aligning day-to-day behaviors with desired outcomes.

The ACT Matrix

The ACT matrix (Polk et al., 2016) is a simple and concrete method that can help coaches and mixed martial artists understand the function of behaviors (e.g., avoidance/escape behavior versus behavior that moves the mixed martial artist toward values) and discriminate between events within the skin (i.e., private events that only you can observe like thoughts) and outside the skin (i.e., what you directly experience, such as a punch being thrown at you).

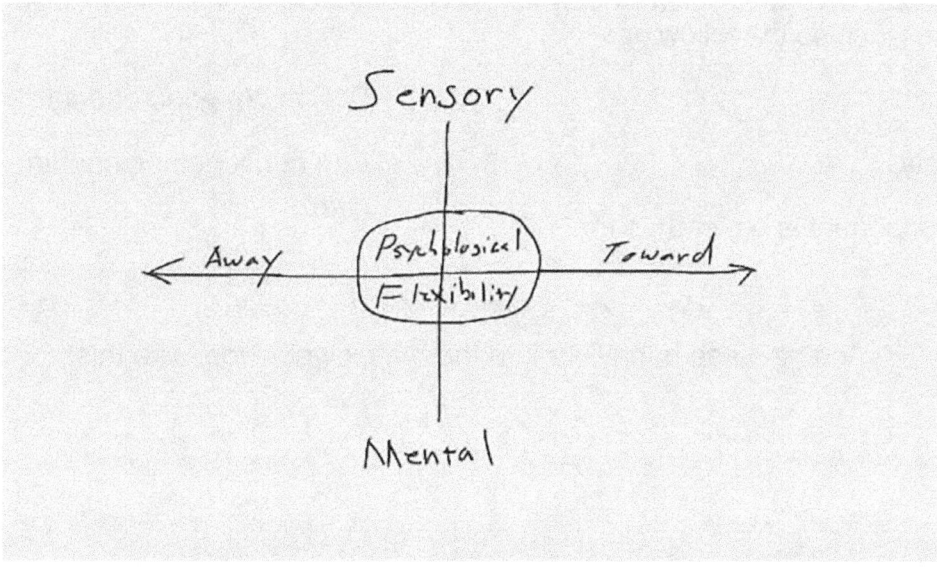

Figure 1. ACT matrix (Polk et al., 2016)

The matrix consists of four quadrants where the mixed martial artist "sorts" behaviors, values, and private events:

1. Who and what you value (lower right quadrant). Examples include the following:

    A. Coach

    B. Teammates

    C. Performing well

    D. Fans

    E. Traveling

    F. Earning income

2. What behaviors will lead you toward the people and things you value (upper right quadrant). Examples include the following:

   A. Training with coach

   B. Engaging in deliberate practice during training and sparring

   C. Doing strength and conditioning

   D. Watching fight videos

   E. Eating healthy food

   F. Going to bed early to rest

   G. Spending time with teammates and coach

3. What behaviors or obstacles lead you away from who or what is important (upper left quadrant) Examples include the following:

   A. Going out and partying

   B. Staying up late

   C. Drinking alcohol

   D. Eating sweets

   E. Straying from game plan when sparring

4. What private events—such as thoughts, feelings, and so on—show up (lower left quadrant). Examples include the following:

   A. Fear

   B. Anxiety

   C. "My opponent is better than me"

   D. "I'm not good enough"

   E. "I'm not getting enough attention in the gym"

   F. "If I lose people won't like me"

Sorting these behaviors into the matrix would look like this:

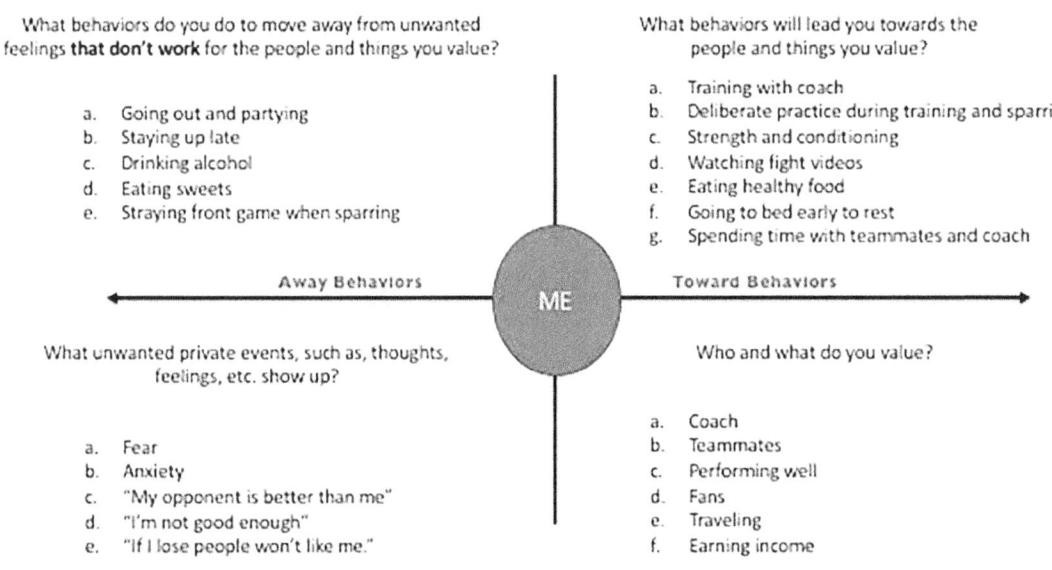

Table 11. On how to sort behaviors into the matrix.

Values and Goals

The easiest way to start thinking about values is to think about who and what is important to you. Of course, you yourself are important, but you probably have family, friends, coaches, and others who are important. In other words, you value them. Spirituality, health, mastery, and community are common values, but notice that the people who are important to you are almost always included in those other values. Of course, in the fight game, many mixed martial artists value performing well, winning a title, earning income, getting fan attention, and perhaps traveling. These can be identified as "what" is important to you.

Goals would then be some concrete thing you could do that would move you toward who and what are important to you. There are long-term goals (e.g., earning a black belt in BJJ) and short-term goals (e.g., learning how to do a Kimura) that lead toward something you value (e.g., winning a title). Short-term goals in relation to who you value might be calling your mom, buying flowers for your sweetheart, saying "thank you" to your coach, or even giving a teammate a high five. While these may seem like simple things, they help propel you toward higher values.

Toward and Away Behavior

Think of how it feels to move toward somebody you care for deeply. Think of how it literally feels to walk toward that person. You probably experience feelings of being liked, being loved, of belonging, and so on. When you successfully move toward another, you feel a sense of satisfaction. These are *toward behaviors*—behaviors that move you toward who and what you value.

Now think of how it feels to move away from fear or pain. If the behavior is successful, then you feel a sense of relief as the fear or pain lessens or goes away. While we all behave in ways that allow us to escape things that may be aversive, sometimes these behaviors are simultaneously moving us away from what we value, as in the examples illustrated in the bottom right corner of the matrix. These are *away behaviors*—behaviors that move you away from who and what you value.

Keep in mind that all humans do a mix of toward and away behaviors every day, and both are necessary for living. The question becomes this: "Did the behavior, either toward or away, work for the life I want to be living?" For the mixed martial artist in fight camp, the "trick" is to find a workable balance of away and toward behaviors that works for winning.

If you practice noticing your toward and away behaviors, you will more quickly notice which ones work for your values and which ones don't. As you deeply notice the ones that work, you will get faster and better at making wise decisions, in both the ring and your life.

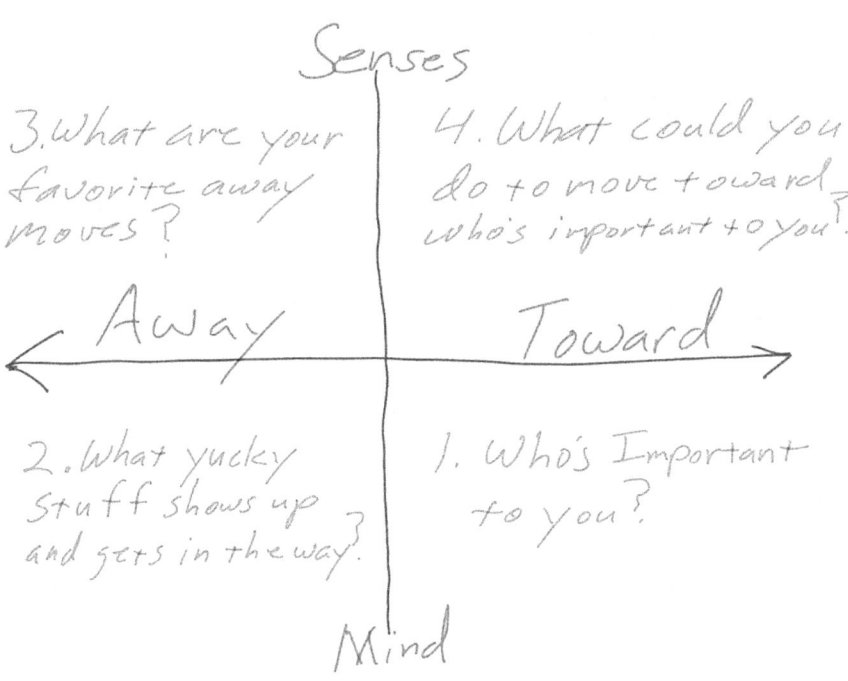

Figure 2. On how to identify values, unwanted private events, and behaviors that move you away and towards your values.

As illustrated in Figure 2, identifying values, unwanted private events, behaviors that move you away from your values, and behaviors that move you towards your values is critical to successful performance. However, it is only part of the formula. You must be become a better observer of your private events and your actions, and be willing to engage in the valued behavior, even when all those negative thoughts and feelings show up.

Psychological Flexibility

By noticing the difference between what's coming in through your senses (behaviors) and what's going on in your mind (the "ME" in the center of the matrix), you can develop what is known as *psychological flexibility*. That simply means that you are able to keep moving or behaving toward who and what's important to you (lower right quadrant) while taking fear, anxiety, and other yucky feelings with you as you move toward what you value (lower left quadrant). Conversely, *psychological inflexibility* is when you keep trying to get rid of the fear, anxiety, and so on instead of just "accepting" it or "taking it with you." Essentially, you end up in a never-ending cycle of unsuccessfully trying to get rid of something that won't go away. You can get more psychologically flexible when you notice the difference between behaviors that lead you toward (satisfaction) your values, and behavior that leads you away (relief) from what you value as a source of temporary relief. Recall how it feels to follow the fight plan outlined by the coach or even help a teammate during their fight camp; that usually leads to satisfaction.

> *You have power over your mind – not outside events.*
> *Realize this, and you will find strength.*
> --
> Marcus Aurelius

Then recall how it feels to move away from fear or anxiety; that usually leads to relief. The simple act of noticing that difference makes you more psychologically flexible. You will be better able to effectively take fear and anxiety with you when you accept rather than fight the feelings and behave in ways that move you toward your goals (e.g., deliberate practice, train with the coach, help your teammates, etc.) Let's look at a simple behavior hack, if you will, for helping you remain psychologically flexible.

Verbal Aikido

You've probably heard of Aikido, the martial art of redirecting physical energy toward peace. Verbal Aikido is when you take the energy of words and direct them toward a peaceful, focused state of awareness within yourself.

Just like a punch coming at you, words have energy. Even when the words show up inside your own mind, they have energy. You feel that energy when someone criticizes you. You also feel that energy when you criticize yourself. You already know how to slip a punch. Even if the punch only misses you by a fraction of an inch, the energy sails right by you. Words are like that—the combat is close; it's within you. Therefore, the best thing a mixed martial artist can do when they are struggling mentally is "slip" or redirect the words, the same way they might "slip" or redirect a punch.

While Verbal Aikido can take some practice, it's a very useful skill that will take the sting out of self-defeating thoughts and keep you at maximum psychological flexibility. All you need to do is set up a "target" to "shoot" the words toward, and then do some target practice. The target is simply the ACT matrix that you already read about earlier. Here's an example:

1. Start by using some words you often use to criticize yourself (e.g., "I'm not good enough").
2. After you think those words, then notice the feeling that shows up inside you.
3. Then ask yourself, "Where do those words go on my matrix? Were the words meant to move me toward or away? If you decided that "I'm not good enough" makes you want to do an away move, then you would write the words in the lower left quadrant. (This is called "sorting into the matrix.")
4. Notice the feeling that shows up inside of you as you sort the words.

It's the same procedure for words coming at you from a person:

1. Notice the words coming at you.
2. Notice the feeling that shows up.
3. Sort the words into a matrix.
4. Notice the feeling that shows up as you sort.

The point here is to notice and accept the words and feelings as opposed to dwelling on them or attempting to suppress them. Attempting to suppress or change your thoughts gets you "hooked," or caught in a vicious and sometimes never-ending loop. After practicing verbal Aikido for a while, you will start to notice a peaceful, focused state of mind showing up. Then you will really be ready for action or *toward behaviors* that will help you reach your goals and values.

Conclusion

In our previous section related to building self-efficacy, we noted that coaches and mixed martial artists can use sources of efficacy (i.e., vicarious learning, verbal persuasion, emotional or physiological states, and mastery experiences) to improve overall confidence and understand that enhancing performance is far more than just training longer and harder. The goal is to become more confident by developing each skill through quality practice, not focusing on an overall sense of confidence. This means focusing on the process and applying each source of efficacy, not focusing on the outcome. Accordingly, the ACT matrix can be used to accelerate both skill and confidence development. The outcome will take care of itself.

CARING FOR THE BODY TO IMPROVE PERFORMANCE

For a mixed martial artist to reach their greatest potential, the connection between mind and body needs to be strong. Accomplishing the different milestones throughout a lifetime of training is more mental than physical. The determination and perseverance to reach a black belt level in MMA is grueling. As such, the way a mixed martial artist takes care of their body is crucial to performance and longevity. Fueling the body with proper nutrition will keep the mixed martial artist physically and mentally prepared for each training session. Imagine the body as a high-powered Formula One race car. Filling this car with regular gas and parts from the local auto shop will never allow this vehicle to perform at its max capacity. Similarly, proper nutrition is like high-octane jet fuel for the body! Strength and conditioning training might be considered the body's monster engine block that powers the mixed martial artist's vehicle. And the skill and technique the mixed martial artist learns is much like the driver navigating those winding city streets at breathtaking speeds. If one of these major components is missing, the ability to compete, train, and learn at one's highest capabilities will be negatively impacted. In the following section, we will provide a brief overview of what macronutrients are and how they act once ingested. As some of these basic concepts are the building blocks of healthy eating, understanding them will allow you to make better-educated decisions about what foods will best fit your goals for a healthy training lifestyle.

We will also cover different types of strength and conditioning, different forms of strength, three major energy systems, and how to develop them. While this information will give the mixed martial artist a very basic foundation for building a quality exercise program, we strongly suggest finding a professional in the fields of both nutrition and strength and conditioning to better assist in the development of a program that works best for your specific goals. Remember, the body and mind work together. They must be fueled correctly to support all of your bodily functions. A healthy brain and body reduce the likelihood you will become injured, which increases your ability to focus on learning, training, and performance improvement.

Nutrition

Nutrition plays a vital role in the success of the mixed martial artist. As such, MMA Science would like to share with you some of the basics of nutrition. This will arm you with a basic understanding of just what macronutrients really do and further prepare you to begin making healthy choices for your MMA lifestyle. It will also give you the baseline knowledge needed to make an educated decision when choosing a diet.

Fats

We will begin with fats. All fats are not made the same. Fats have about 9 calories per gram and help our bodies absorb vitamins and minerals. They also help build cell membranes. Fats are essential for blood clotting, muscular movement, and inflammation. Below is a breakdown of the different types of fats.

Trans fats are the worst type of fats for the human body. They are produced through a process called hydrogenation and have no known health benefits. Trans fats have been banned in the United States since 2015.

Saturated fats are commonly found in red meat, whole milk, cheese, and coconut oil. Saturated fat is solid at room temperature. Saturated fat has a bad history and was once demonized. However, notably, there are a variety of new studies that have determined there is no link between saturated fats and increased risk of heart disease.

Monounsaturated fats and polyunsaturated fats are considered good fats. These fats are mainly found in nuts, seeds, and fish; they remain in liquid form at room temperature.

Polyunsaturated fats are essential fats. They are needed for our body functions to perform correctly. These fats are used for building cell membranes and covering nerves.

Omega 3 fatty acids are known for their anti-inflammatory properties and may help reduce the risk of heart disease and stroke. Good sources of these fats are fatty fish such as salmon and mackerel. Nuts and seeds are also good sources.

Omega 6 fatty acids are also linked to protection from heart disease. These fats are commonly found in foods with high linoleic acid, such as safflower and sunflower oils.

Carbohydrates

Carbohydrates have about 4 calories per gram. Carbohydrates provide the body with glucose, which is converted to energy for body functions and physical activity. Choosing the best source of carbohydrates is most important no matter what diet you follow. Eating whole foods like whole grains, quinoa, and sweet potato are much better options than refined white breads or fried potatoes. Good sources of carbohydrates deliver vitamins, minerals, fiber, and phytonutrients, which support healthy body functions and improved performance. Bad carbohydrate choices, such as highly processed and refined foods, can cause weight gain, promote diabetes and heart disease, and negatively impact performance. The general rule of thumb is that the leaner the mixed martial artist is, the better. Choosing carbohydrates that do not support healthy body functions can negatively impact your fat percentage and be devastating at many different levels.

Protein

Protein has about 4 calories per gram and is found in virtually every part of the human body, from muscle to skin and hair. Protein is made from a chain of 20 plus amino acids, and the human body can make or convert all but nine of these. The remaining nine, known as essential amino acids, are histidine, isoleucine, leucine, lysine, methionine, phenylalanine, threonine, and valine. These nine essential amino acids must come from meat, eggs, cheese, poultry, quinoa, and buckwheat. Here, quality of food matters, so try to eat grass-fed meat, free-range organic chicken, and wild-caught seafood. Amino acids have been linked to improved athletic performance, increased lean muscle mass, and improved sleep—all of which are vital for the success of the mixed martial artist.

Hydration

Hydration might be the most important thing that regularly and immediately impacts the mixed martial artist's performance. Approximately 60% of the human body is made up of water, and humans lose water through sweating, breathing, and using the restroom. Research has shown that as little as 2% of body weight lost in exercise can negatively affect performance. Decreased water in the body means decreased blood volume, and decreased blood volume affects many major functions in the body. When the mixed martial artist is dehydrated, less blood is pumped with each heartbeat. This causes muscles to receive less oxygen, and the bad biproducts of exercise cannot be flushed out, which accelerates exhaustion and increases the likelihood of injury. To stay hydrated throughout the day, do not wait until you're thirsty to drink water. Drink plenty of water before, during, and after your workout. Two easy ways to monitor your hydration is through weight and urine. Weigh yourself before and after a workout. Be sure to replace the body weight lost with food and water, and regularly monitor the color of your urine. Urine should remain clear to pale yellow at all times as this represents a hydrated mixed martial artist. When urine becomes dark yellow or brown, it represents a very dehydrated mixed martial artist and can be a sign of bigger problems.

Muscle Fibers and MMA

There are three types of muscle fibers in the body. They are categorized by how fast they work and how they provide ATP (energy). The first type is slow oxidative or type 1 fibers. These are also referred to as *red fibers*. They are called red fibers because the blood they hold in them gives them a red color. These fibers use the aerobic system to contract, slowly, and cannot produce very much force. As a result, they are used mainly for things like postural stability and running marathons. Think long, slow exercise. Although, all three energy systems are working throughout the fight simultaneously, the aerobic system is dominate during continuous work across 15-25 minutes intervals. In MMA, building an aerobic base is critical to successful performance. A solid aerobic base can typically be achieved by keeping your heart rate between 50-70% of your max for approximately 30 –60 min. As long as you stay within these parameters, aerobic capacity can be improved by running, heavy bag work, shadow boxing, grappling and swimming. If you see a significant decrease in overall output over the course of the fight, the aerobic system might be the energy system that needs improvement.

Fast oxidative fibers or type 2a, otherwise known as *white fibers*, use oxygen to convert glucose to ATP (energy). They contract fast but switch to the anaerobic system. Consequently, they fatigue much faster than type 1 fibers. These might be thought of as middle-ground fibers that include both type 1 and type 2a fibers. Where type 1 fibers would be dominate in a marathon, in MMA, type 2a fibers would be dominate during multiple takedown attempts, scrambles and clinching that lasts approximately 30 seconds to 2 minutes. Training to improve conditioning in this zone can be done by reaching a heart rate of 80-90% for approximately 90 seconds. Training position specific scenarios is great way to build this system. For example, escaping or replacing guard from side control. Once the goal is accomplished or the time limit is met, the round is over. Repeat the drill for multiple rounds with adequate recovery while engaging in 80-90% effort each round.

Fast glycolytic type 2b fibers have the fastest contractions of all three fiber types. These fibers use anaerobic glycolysis to produce ATP (energy), produce the most force, but fatigue the fastest. Type 2b fibers would be most dominate during techniques like short burst, powerful combinations, or when driving through a takedown. Training this system is done at 95-100% of your heart rate for 10 seconds or less with adequate recovery to reach 95-100% effort on each round. Training to improve this energy system is most popular through sprinting.

Some of you might be wondering why we mentioned both heart rate and effort. The fact is, not everybody has access to heart rate monitors; however, everybody *can* gauge their own effort. While assigning a percentage to your own effort might not be as precise, it can provide a powerful source of measurement through regular self-monitoring.

Knowing which energy system is dominate during different aspects of training or fighting provides the martial artist with the opportunity to more accurately analyze why they might be failing to perform at an acceptable level; moreover, it provides the opportunity for increased precision during training to achieve better performance outcomes.

Ultimately, good nutrition and hydration provide the high-octane fuel needed to accelerate performance. But even with the best training, coaching, and nutrition, the body still needs to be prepared for the stressors associated with combat. This requires the mixed martial artist to engage in healthy strength and conditioning programs. Let's take a deeper below.

Strength and Conditioning

Strength and conditioning are how a mixed martial artist builds a big engine to perform every day. Not all strength is built the same, though. In this section, MMA science will break down the building blocks, so you can better understand how the different types of strength work.

Maximal strength is the absolute max amount of weight an athlete can lift. Maximal strength is best tested by exercises that are one rep max. Further, maximal strength is most effectively built by working with heavy weights and very low repetitions. To maximize strength and return on investment, weight should be within 80%–100% of the mixed martial artist's one-rep max. Examples of exercises used for building max-effort strength include the squat, bench press, and deadlift.

Strength speed is often used interchangeably with speed strength. This is a misconception. Strength speed is its very own type of strength and is found on the strength continuum. Strength speed is defined as moving relatively heavy weights as fast as possible. This type of strength is trained at 60%–75% of the athlete's one-rep max. Olympic-style lifts are often used to develop this type of strength.

Speed strength is defined as force X distance divided by time. This is power. Speed strength is normally trained around 40%–60% of the athlete's one-rep max. Exercises that can be used to develop this type of strength are weighted jump variations, Olympic-style lifts, and medicine-ball throw variations.

Speed itself is the ability to move quickly across the mat or ground, or move limbs rapidly to strike or grapple. Speed requires good strength, power, and the mixed martial artist to be at their optimal weight. Further, speed is found at the opposite end of the strength continuum from maximal strength. Speed testing has been made famous by the NFL combine's 40-yard sprint. Training absolute speed is done with no weights, and exercises that are commonly used to increase speed are jumping and sprinting.

> *Fatigue makes cowards of us all.*
> --
> George S. Patton Jr.

Cardio respiratory endurance is a measurement of how well your heart, lungs, and muscles work together during exercise. The three main energy systems affecting this endurance are the phosphagen system, anaerobic glycolysis, and aerobic glycolysis. The phosphagen system uses creatine phosphate to create energy. This energy is instantly available and used in the start of exercise. The phosphagen system energy only lasts for about 30 seconds during high-intensity work, such as sprinting. Anaerobic glycolysis does not require oxygen to produce energy and is the immediate pathway between the phosphagen and aerobic systems. This system will support energy from about 30 seconds to 3 minutes, after which the aerobic system picks up. Aerobic glycolysis uses oxygen to burn carbohydrates and fats, which produces the energy needed for longer low-level bouts of exercise. The three energy systems of the body are always working together to produce the energy needed. One system will become more dominant over the others based on the length and intensity of the activity. A mixed martial artist needs to work in all aspects of the strength continuum. Speed, power, and strength will help the mixed martial artist's striking, wrestling, and grappling. The ability to move quickly, drive through takedowns, and strike with speed and power relies heavily on how much the mixed martial artist has focused on strength and conditioning. The mixed martial artist will find themselves using all three energy systems throughout a fight or training. To maximize their potential, then, the mixed martial artist must train in all three aspects. Knowing the technique and having strength, however, are meaningless if the brain and muscles are supplied with insufficient oxygen. If the mixed martial artist is deficient in any area—in strength, cardiorespiratory health, or nutrition—the deficiency will have a negative effect on learning, training, competition, and self-defense. For that reason, MMA Science recommends finding a strength and conditioning specialist who can make a safe and effective program specifically geared toward the needs of the martial artist.

FINAL THOUGHTS

To this point, we have provided you, the mixed martial arts student or coach, with the formula for accelerating success. Just remember, it's not about quantity, but quality. Bruce Lee summed this up perfectly when he said, "I fear not the man who has practiced 10,000 kicks once, but I fear the man who has practiced one kick 10,000 times." Great mixed martial artists engage in quality reps along with other aspects of training, including good coaching and sparring. As you know, an important component of deliberate practice, as highlighted in BST, is for the mixed martial artist to continually receive performance feedback through deliberate coaching, and this includes self-coaching. For example, you might watch yourself in the mirror for immediate feedback or film yourself shadowboxing or drilling a grappling technique. Such feedback provides coaches and students an opportunity to review the video and make any necessary corrections based on the feedback. When doing this, you should use the task analysis provided by MMA Science as a tool for evaluating your own performance. Importantly, the MMA student must regularly recruit and accept the feedback and then integrate it into their deliberate practice. Good feedback is a gift. When the MMA student fails to act on feedback, they are wasting a valuable resource that will allow them to improve. Accordingly, we leave you with this: Don't waste your time as a student or coach. Learn to recruit, accept, and deliver feedback as all learning requires it. If you do this, you will excel as a mixed martial artist!

SKILL ANALYSIS & PERFORMANCE SCORECARDS

International Mixed Martial Arts Ranking System:

YELLOW BELT

INTRODUCTION

Tradition

MMA, considered a combat sport as the martial artist learns what works in the cage or ring, has lacked other aspects of development linked to physical, mental, emotional, and spiritual development. Until now. MMA Science brings tradition back to martial arts through virtues rooted in Bushido, which translates into "way of the warrior." An ethical system, Bushido is a code of conduct that advocates behaviors associated with frugality, righteousness, courage, benevolence, respect, sincerity, honor, loyalty, and self-control. Following the etiquette and traditions associated with the martial arts like wearing uniforms and bowing fosters a sense of respect for the coach and students within the gym that reflective of the Bushido values that generalize into the martial artist's daily personal and professional life.

Organization

In Asian tradition, the color white can symbolize simplicity or purity, and the color black can symbolize depth or greater knowledge. As such, belt systems represent the progression of knowledge as each belt color represents various stages of growth and development. At MMA Science we are very proud to bring the first ever belt ranking system to mixed martial arts. While the purpose of color belts is to signify the level of experience in martial arts its wearer has achieved, it also allows the coaches to more precisely structure their classes around the needs of the learners. Through an organized curriculum that builds belt ranks off the fundamentals, our step-by-step descriptions, pictures, and videos allows mixed martial arts coaches and students to immediately put our system into action regardless of their experience. Moreover, our system offers a simple measurement process that allows coaches to objectively measure each technique during preparation or testing. The result, accelerated learning through an organized and transparent path to achieving belts that can be proudly worn through a variety of clothing options

Science

MMA Science has broken down the most effective techniques commonly used in MMA into specific behaviors so they can be easily taught and practiced to a level of proficiency. This is what is called a task analysis. Over the course of this practice, a constant stream of positive and corrective feedback from a coach can accelerate learning and performance. MMA Science recommends coaches use Behavior Skills Training (BST), rooted in behavior science, BST includes instruction, modeling, rehearsal, and feedback to reinforce or "shape" incremental improvements towards a desired skill. Once a fighter is able to demonstrate a skill independently, we recommend the martial artist continue to practice a striking or grappling technique many times and over progressively more challenging conditions in order for him or her to become "fluent" as evidenced by techniques occurring quickly, precisely, and automatically during combat conditions. Once a skill is mastered, this "fluency training" as it is known to the science of human behavior adds the all-important speed criterion so that fighters can respond accurately and without hesitation when the opportunity presents itself.

One of the benefits of having a task analysis of each skill as supplied by MMA Science is that a martial artist who doesn't always have the benefit of a coach can "self-coach" if you will by using a combination of the video modeling and task analysis to monitor and correct their own performance based on the standards provided. As a coach or a student, even if you do not understand all the science behind training, you should know that learning is a process that builds on fundamentals. Whether you are learning or coaching, MMA Science is presenting you with a structured task analysis that builds upon itself and will allow you to measurably accelerate learning and performance.

Paul Gavoni   David Zitnick   Roger Krahl

Yellow Belt Skillset

		Offense and Positioning	Defense and Positioning
Striking		MMA Stance	Basic Head Movement
		Jab	Linear foot work
		Cross	Lateral Foot Work
		Straight Knee (step)	Parry jab
		Rear Leg Push kick	Block Cross
		Lead Leg Front kick	Block Straight Knee
			Block Rear Leg Push Kick
			Block Lead Leg Push Kick
Grappling		Underhook	Basic Bridging
		Overhook	Bridge and Reach
		Pummeling	Bridge and Roll
		Body Lock	Bridge and Shrimp
		Collar tie	Full Guard Bottom
		Full Guard Top	Half Guard Bottom
		Basic Double leg	Technical MMA Get Up
		Half Guard Top	

YELLOW BELT

MMA Stance

Description: The MMA stance is a *fundamental technique* focuses as it is central to many other areas related to offensive and defensive techniques. *Fundamental techniques* open up a person's repertoire across situations.

1. Rear Foot Placement	Rear foot natural step back, 45 degrees, slightly raised
2. Front Foot Placement	Slightly toed in, flat
3. Foot Spacing	Feet approximately shoulder width apart
4. Balance	Weight equally distributed
5. Knees	Slightly bent
6. Body Orientation	Approximately 45 degrees
7. Back Position	Vertical to slightly forward
8. Elbow Position	Elbows close to body, pointed down
9. Hand Height	Hands raised to approximately cheek level with eye gaze slightly above hands
10. Head Positioning	Chin slightly down

Pictures

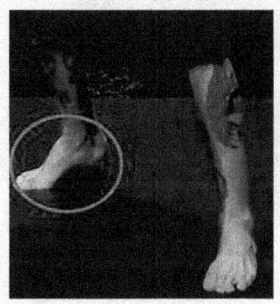 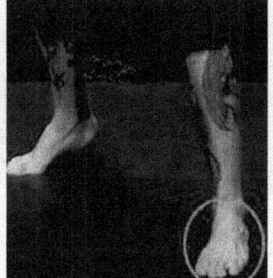  

Your Notes:

Lateral Footwork	
Description: Footwork is a *pivotal technique* focuses as it is central to many areas related to offensive and defensive techniques. *Pivotal techniques* provide opportunities for improvement in other techniques and associated desired outcomes.	
1 Lead side Step	Push off the ball of the rear foot, lift the lead foot and take half step sideways
2. Lead Step Back Foot	Rear foot follows and moves equal distance sideways
3. Feet Spacing	Feet return to original foot spacing
4. Rear Side Step Back Foot	Push off the ball of the lead foot, lift the rear foot and take half step sideways
5. Rear Step Front Foot	Lead foot follows and moves equal distance sideways
6. Feet Spacing	Feet return to original foot spacing
7. Stance	All elements of stance maintained

Pictures

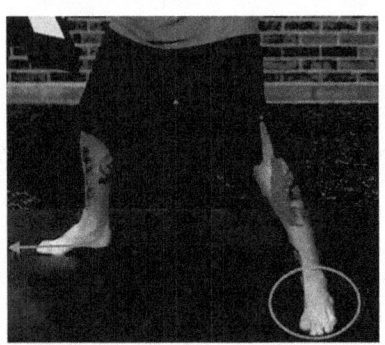 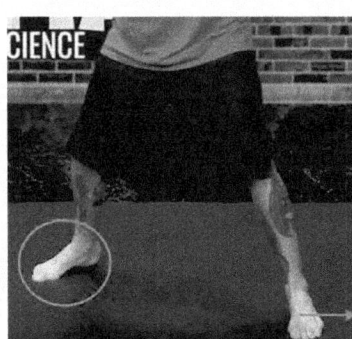 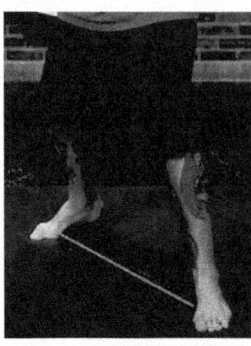

Your Notes:

Linear Footwork

Description: Footwork is a *pivotal technique* focuses as it is central to many areas related to offensive and defensive techniques. *Pivotal techniques* provide opportunities for improvement in other techniques and associated desired outcomes.

1. Advancing Step Front Foot	Push off the ball of the rear foot, lift the lead foot and take half step forward
2. Advancing Step Back Foot	Rear foot follows and moves equal distance forward
3. Feet Spacing	Feet return to original foot spacing
4. Retreating Back Foot	Push off the ball of the lead foot, lift the rear foot and take half step backwards
5. Retreating Step Front Foot	Lead foot follows and moves equal distance backwards
6. Feet Spacing	Feet return to original foot spacing
7. Stance	All elements of stance maintained

Pictures

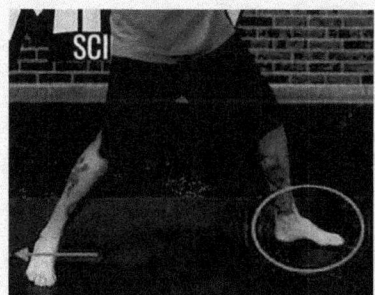  

Your Notes:

Basic Head Movement

Description: Head movement is a *pivotal technique* focuses as it is central to many areas related to offensive and defensive techniques. *Pivotal techniques* provide opportunities for improvement in other techniques and associated desired outcomes.

1. Rear foot head movement	Trunk rotates slightly towards the rear foot
2. Rear foot balance	Balance shifts slightly towards the rear foot
3. Rear Head Movement	Head shifts slightly off center line towards the rear foot
4. Return to stance	Trunk and head return to stance
5. Lead foot head movement	Trunk rotates slightly towards the lead foot
6. Lead foot balance	Balance shifts slightly towards the lead foot
7. Lead head movement	Head shifts slightly off center towards the lead foot
8. Level change head movement	Bend knees, head lowers below chest level
9. Stance	All elements of stance maintained

Pictures

Your Notes:

Jab

Description: The jab is a *pivotal technique* focuses as it is central to many areas related to offensive and defensive techniques. *Pivotal techniques* provide opportunities for improvement in other techniques and associated desired outcomes.

1. Stance:	All elements of MMA stance in place
2. Advancing Step Front Foot	Push off the ball of the rear foot, lift the lead foot and take half step forward
3. Strike	Propel lead hand from MMA stance ballistically forward with rear hand held at temple
4. Advancing Step Back Foot	Rear foot follows and moves equal distance forward
5. Feet Spacing	Feet return to original foot spacing
6. Retreating Back Foot	Push off the ball of the lead foot, lift the rear foot and take half step backwards
7. Retreating Step Front Foot	Lead foot follows and moves equal distance backwards
8. Feet Spacing	Feet return to original foot spacing
9. Stance	Return to MMA stance

Pictures

Your Notes:

Parry Jab

Description: The jab is a *pivotal technique* focuses as it is central to many areas related to offensive and defensive techniques. *Pivotal techniques* provide opportunities for improvement in other techniques and associated desired outcomes.

1. Stance:	All elements of MMA stance in place
2. Hand	Deflects incoming jab using an open palm by moving the hand approximately 6-12 inches in sweeping downward motion
3. Elbow	Parrying hand elbow and all other elements of MMA stance remains static
4. Return	Hand returns to the original position

Pictures

Your Notes:

Cross

Description: The cross is a *pivotal technique* focuses as it is central to many areas related to offensive and defensive techniques. *Pivotal techniques* provide opportunities for improvement in other techniques and associated desired outcomes.

1. Stance:	All elements of MMA stance in place
2. Hips:	Rotate to hips forward to a 90 degree angle
3. Rear Pivot:	Pivot the rear foot from 45 to a 90 degree angle and shift weight to lead foot
4. Strike:	Propel the rear hand from the cheek ballisticly forward with lead hand held at temple
5. Knuckles Down:	Rotate the knuckles down upon full extension
6. Stance:	Return to MMA stance

Pictures

Your Notes:

Block Cross

Description: Blocking is a *pivotal technique* focuses as it is central to many areas related to offensive and defensive techniques. *Pivotal techniques* provide opportunities for improvement in other techniques and associated desired outcomes.

1. Stance	All elements of MMA stance in place
2. Hands	Using an open or closed fist, slightly raise the hand and secure it to the head near the temple
3. Torso	Rotate torso slightly in the same direction the cross is moving to absorb cross
4. Elbow	Elbow remains pointed towards the ground and close to body
5. Return	Return to MMA Stance

Pictures

Your Notes:

Lead Leg Front Kick

Description: The lead front is a basic strike that pairs the snap of the lower leg with the knee raised and the thrust of the hips to deliver moderate and long range power with the lead leg. To be effective, distance must be precise and the knee must be brought up quickly. Knees, straight kicks, and round kicks all use the same basic line of attack.

1. Stance	All elements of MMA stance in place
2. Rear Pivot	Step rear foot from 45 degree angle to match distance to target
3. Strike	Explosively drive knee of front leg towards target then thrust ball of foot through target
4. Hips	Explosively drive hips forward toward target as upper body shifts slightly back
5. Upper body	Rear hand at temple and lead hand projects forward with thumb side down and fingers turned inside while keeping chin behind front shoulder
6. Stance	Return to MMA stance

Pictures

Your Notes:

Rear Leg Front Kick

Description: Similar to the lead front kick, the rear leg front kick is a basic strike that pairs the snap of the lower leg with the knee raised and thrust of the hips to deliver moderate and long range power with the rear leg. To be effective, distance must be precise and the knee must be brought up quickly. Knees, straight kicks, and round kicks all use the same basic line of attack.

1. Stance	All elements of MMA stance in place
2. Rear Pivot	Pivot the rear foot from a 45 to a 90 degree angle
3. Hips	Rotate hips forward to a 90 degree angle
4. Strike	Explosively drive knee towards target then thrust ball of foot through target
5. Lead Pivot	Pivot the heel of the front foot to an inside 45 degree angle
6. Hips	Explosively drive hips forward toward target as upper body shifts slightly back
7. Hands	Lead hand at temple and rear hand projects forward with thumb side down and fingers turned inside while keeping chin behind rear shoulder
8. Stance	Return to MMA stance

Pictures

Your Notes:

Lead Leg Front Kick Defense

Description: The Lead leg front kick defense involves the martial artists parrying with the hands. To avoid compromising defense, the martial artist should use the opposite side hand to parry the kick while sweeping the kick in a downward motion to keep the opponent out of position and avoid counters.

1. Stance	All elements of MMA stance in place
2. Rear Foot	Step outside angle 45 degrees
3. Upper Body	Lead hand sweeps outside lead leg while shoulder covers chin and rear hand held at temple
4. Hips	Pivot hips inside to 90 degrees
5. Lead Foot	Immediately follow rear foot back to 45 degrees
6. Stance	Return to MMA stance

Pictures

Your Notes:

Rear Leg Front Kick Defense

Description: The Rear leg front kick defense involves the martial artists parrying with the hands. To avoid compromising defense, the martial artist should use the opposite side hand to parry the kick while sweeping the kick in a downward motion to keep the opponent out of position and avoid counters.

1. Stance	All elements of MMA stance in place
2. Lead Foot	Lead foot steps up angle 45 degrees and pivots inside 45 degrees
3. Upper Body	Lead hand sweeps inside lead leg simultaneously as lead shoulder covers chin and rear hand held at temple
4. Hips	Pivot hips inside 45 degrees
5. Rear Foot	Immediately follow lead foot up to 45 degrees
6. Stance	Return to MMA stance

Pictures

Your Notes:

Full Guard Top

Description: Full Guard Top is a *fundamental technique* focuses as it is central to all other areas related to offensive and defensive techniques. *Fundamental techniques* open up a person's repertoire across situations.

1. Knees	Knees wider than shoulder width
2. Feet	Tops of feet flat to ground or toes engaged.
3. Buttocks	Buttocks sits tightly to the heals
4. Posture	Body lean is approx. 45 degrees
5. Hands	Hand position is on biceps or arm pits
6. Elbows	Point of elbows is kept rotated towards y our body. (Not facing out)
7. Head	Head position is neutral with chin slightly tucked.

Pictures

Your Notes:

Full Guard Bottom

Description: Full Guard Bottom is a *fundamental technique* focuses as it is central to many other areas related to offensive and defensive techniques on the ground. *Fundamental techniques* open up a person's repertoire across situations.

1. Legs	Legs are locked around opponent's waist line. Above hips
2. Knees	Knees are squeezed tight against the ribs
3. Hands	Hands are high protecting chin or on opponents' biceps/armpits.
4. Head	Head position is chin tucked with back of head lifted off the ground.
5. Shoulders	Shoulders raised slightly off the matt

Pictures

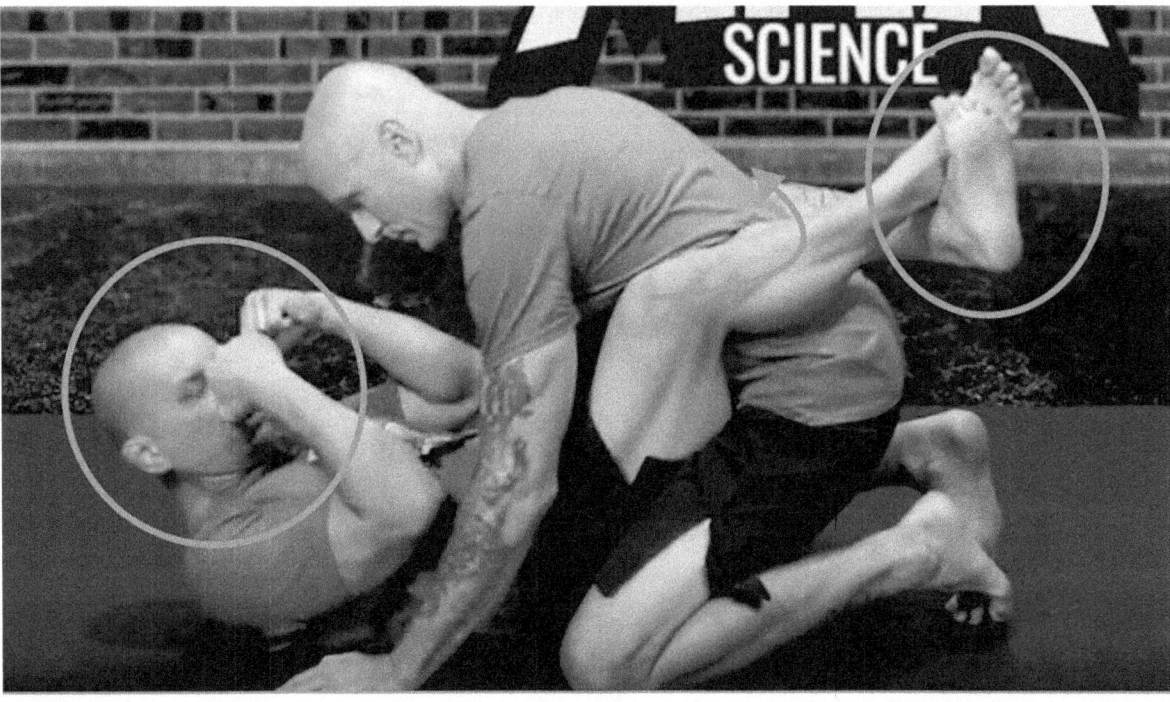

Your Notes:

Basic Bridge

Description: The Basic Bridge is a *fundamental technique* focuses as it is central to all other areas related to offensive and defensive techniques on the ground. *Fundamental techniques* open up a person's repertoire across situations.

1. Head	Head flat to the ground
2. Torso	Torso flat to the ground
3. Feet	Bottom of feet flat on the ground pulled close to buttocks
4. Knees	Pointed up
5. Hands	Elbows tight to body, palms facing each other
6. Hips	Ballistically elevate hips vertically
7. Return	Return to original body positioning

Pictures

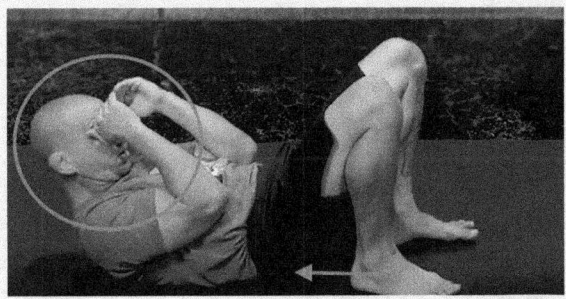 

Your Notes

Bridge and Reach

Description: The Bridge and Reach is a pivotal technique focuses as it is central to many areas related to offensive and defensive techniques. Pivotal techniques provide opportunities for improvement in other techniques and associated desired outcomes.

1. Head	Head flat to the ground
2. Torso	Torso flat to the ground
3. Feet	Bottom of feet flat on the ground pulled close to buttocks
4. Knees	Pointed up
5. Hands	Elbows tight to body, palms facing each other
6. Hips	Ballistically elevate hips diagonally towards one shoulder
7. Arm	Extend arm fully over the shoulder in the same direction hips are moving
8. Return	Return to original body positioning

Pictures

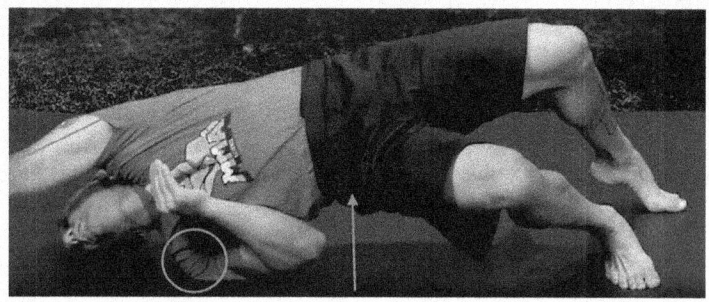

Your Notes:

Bridge and Roll

Description: The Bridge and Roll is a pivotal technique focuses as it is central to many areas related to offensive and defensive techniques. Pivotal techniques provide opportunities for improvement in other techniques and associated desired outcomes.

1. Head	Head flat to the ground
2. Torso	Torso flat to the ground
3. Feet	Bottom of feet flat on the ground pulled close to buttocks
4. Knees	Pointed up
5. Hands	Elbows tight to body, palms facing each other
6. Hips	Ballistically elevate hips diagonally towards one shoulder
7. Arm	Extend arm fully over the shoulder in the same direction hips are moving
8. Legs	Using the leg on the same side as reaching hand, kick leg over the hips rotating the torso down as the palm of your reaching hand is placed flat on the ground
9. Hand	Remaining hand is placed flat on the ground
10. Finish	Hands and knees are on the ground with tops of feet flat to ground or toes engaged.

Pictures

Your Notes:

Bridge and Shrimp		
Description: The Bridge and Shrimp is a pivotal technique focuses as it is central to many areas related to offensive and defensive techniques. Pivotal techniques provide opportunities for improvement in other techniques and associated desired outcomes.	
1. Head	Head flat to the ground
2. Torso	Torso flat to the ground
3. Feet	Bottom of feet flat on the ground pulled close to buttocks
4. Knees	Pointed up
5. Hands	Elbows tight to body, palms facing each other
6. Hips	Ballistically elevate hips vertically
7. Torso	Rotate torso down to either side until the shoulder and foot on that side are the only areas of the body touching the ground
8. Foot	Keep foot planted on the ground and move hips away from feet
9. Arms/Legs	Arms and legs are fully extended
10. Return	Return to basic bridge position

Pictures

Your Notes:

Technical MMA Get Up

Description: The MMA Technical get up allows the martial artist to transition safely from a prone to stand up position. A key to this movement is keeping the torso postured and avoid leaning head down and forward as this is exposes the martial artist to a variety of offensive techniques from the opponent.

1. Position	Begin in the Basic Bridge position
2. Bridge/shrimp	Bridge and shrimp*
3. Hip*	Hip remains on the ground and bottom of the foot remains facing forward
4. Sit up	Sit up to elbow on same side as hip touching ground
5. Arm	Place opposite arm straight out forming a straight line from hand to opposite elbow
6. Elbow	Replace grounded elbow with hand while opposite arm remains in a straight line
7. Hips	Hips are elevated off the floor
8. Foot	Foot sweeps in a C type motion from the front to the rear
9. Head	Head remains vertical to the ground through the sweeping motion
10. Finish	Finishes in MMA Stance

Pictures

Your Notes:

Rear Knee

Description: The straight knee can be thrown from a short to mid-range position with the target generally the top of the abdomen or the opponent's head under the right conditions. To gain power with the straight knee the martial artist must incorporate a thrusting upward and forward motion with the hips. Knees, straight kicks, and round kicks all use the same basic line of attack.

1. Stance	All elements of MMA stance in place
2. Rear pivot	Rear Pivot - pivot the rear foot from a 45 to a 90 degree angle
3. Hips	Rotate hips forward to a 90 degree angle
4. Strike	Explosively drive knee pointed to target with foot tucked underneath
5. Front pivot	Pivot the heel of the front foot to an inside 45 degree angle
6. Hips	Explosively drive hips forward towards target as upper body shifts slightly back
7. Upper Body	Lead hand held at temple and rear hand projects forward with thumb side down and fingers turned inside while keeping chin behind rear shoulder
8. Stance	Return to MMA stance

Pictures

Your Notes:

Rear Knee Defense

Description: The basic rear knee defense involves the martial artist using footwork to avoid the direct knee while simultaneously using the elbow and high guard to deflect the knee and set up a counter.

1. Stance	All elements of MMA stance in place
2. Lead foot	Lead foot steps up angle 45 degrees
3. Upper body	Lead elbow angles into attacking knee at 45 degree angle with outside of pinky finger facing attacking knee, rear hand held at temple
4. Rear foot	Immediately follows front foot up angle 45 degrees
5. Hips	Explosively pivot hips from a 90 degree angle to a 45 degree angle inside
6. Stance	Return to MMA stance

Pictures

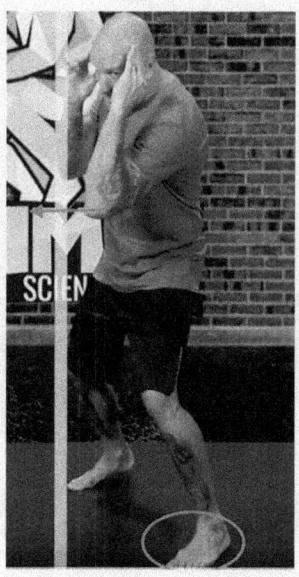

Your Notes:

Underhook

Description: The Underhook is a pivotal technique focuses as it is central to many areas related to offensive and defensive techniques. Pivotal techniques provide opportunities for improvement in other techniques and associated desired outcomes.

1. Stance	Begin from an MMA Stance
2. Hand	Reach hand through opponents arm pit
3. Leg	Leg steps forward simultaneously as hand reaches through arm pit
4. Grip	Grip back of the opponent's shoulder
5. Elbow	Elbow is pulled in tight towards the body
6. Head	Forehead is pushing into the neck of the opponent
7. Knees	Knees are slightly bent

Pictures

Your Notes:

Overhook

Description: The Overhook is a pivotal technique focuses as it is central to many areas related to offensive and defensive techniques. Pivotal techniques provide opportunities for improvement in other techniques and associated desired outcomes.

1. Stance	Begin from MMA Stance and opponent has underhook position
2. Grip	Hand on tricep using a C-Grip
3. Elbow**	Elbow is locked tight to the body
4. Head	Forehead is pushing into the neck of the opponent
5. Knees	Knees are slightly bent

Pictures

Your Notes:

Pummeling

Description: Pummeling is a pivotal technique focuses as it is central to many areas related to offensive and defensive techniques. Pivotal techniques provide opportunities for improvement in other techniques and associated desired outcomes.

1. Stance	Being with one underhook* and one overhook*, chest to chest, with underhook leg forward
2. Swim hands	Simultaneously use underhook and overhook skills to alternate hand and body and positioning

Pictures

 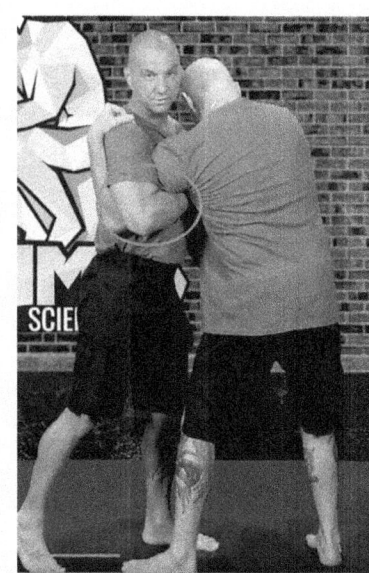

Your Notes:

Body Lock

Description: The body lock is a pivotal technique focuses as it is central to many areas related to offensive and defensive techniques. Pivotal techniques provide opportunities for improvement in other techniques and associated desired outcomes. A body lock offers the martial artist direct control over the opponent from the front, rear, or side.

1. Double Underhook	Begin from Double Underhook* position
2. Grips	Grip hands in preferred grip (e.g. gable grip, S grip, butterfly grip)
3. Elbows	Elbows pointed down and pressed tight to the opponent
4. Foot	Step either foot behind opponent
5. Hips	Turn hips perpendicular to the opponents
6. Knees	Bend knees to lower hips just below that of the opponents
7. Head	Head pressed tight to opponent's chest
8. Head to Chest	Simultaneously push head to the chest while steering back elbow towards the ground
9. Finish	Drive opponent to the ground with hips down and chest up with body tight to opponent

Pictures

Your Notes:

Collar Tie	
Description: The Collar Tie is a pivotal technique focuses as it is central to many areas related to offensive and defensive techniques. Pivotal techniques provide opportunities for improvement in other techniques and associated desired outcomes.	
1. MMA Stance	All elements of MMA Stance* in place
2. Arms	Extend arm towards opponent with arm remaining at approximately a 90 degree angle
3. Forearm	Forearm remains vertical as it presses into opponent's neck
4. Elbow	Elbow is pressed into center of opponent's chest
5. Hand	Hand grips "crown" area on back of head
Pictures	

Your Notes

Half Guard Bottom

Description: The Half Guard Bottom is a pivotal technique focuses as it is central to many areas related to offensive and defensive techniques. Pivotal techniques provide opportunities for improvement in other techniques and associated desired outcomes.

1. Leg	Legs are locked in a "figure 4" around one of the opponent's legs as evidenced by the ankle of one foot fitting tightly to the inside of the opposite knee
2. Hands	One hand frames collar bone; the opposite hand controls bicep
3. Hips	Torso is turned towards the opponent with weight distributed to the hip closest to the opponent
4. Shoulders	Shoulders raised slightly off the matt

Pictures

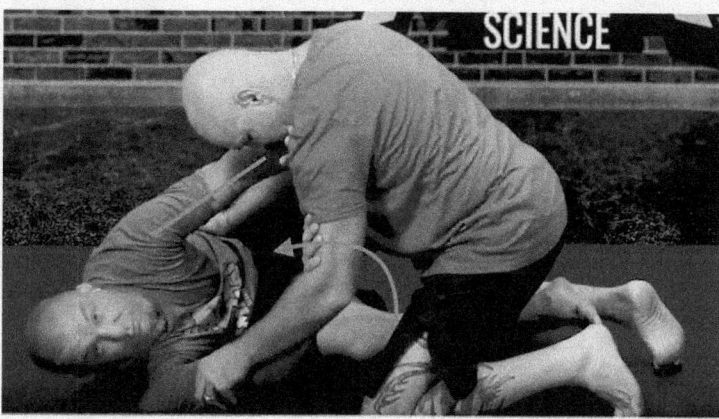

Your Notes:

Basic Double Leg

Description: The basic double leg takedown is a high percentage takedown that involves dropping level to shoot in and grab the opponent with both arms around the legs, chest close to opponent, using the shot momentum to force the opponent to the ground. The double leg is most effectively applied when strikes are used to set it up.

1. MMA Stance	All elements of MMA Stance* in place
2. Hips	Bend knees to lower hips below the hips of the opponents
3. Advancing Step Front Foot	Push off the ball of the rear foot, lift the lead foot and take half step forward.
4. Body	Upper body remains in MMA stance and propels ballistically towards the opponent
5. Hands	Hands reach behind and grip the back of the opponent's knees
6. Elbows	Elbows pressed tight to the outside of opponent's mid-thigh
7. Foot	Rear footsteps parallel to lead foot on the outside of opponent's leg
8. Hips	Hips are close to opponent's body as possible
9. Head	Head is above hips pressed tightly to side of torso with eye gaze pointing up and in
10. Finish	Run through opponent landing on ground with hips down and chest up with body tight to opponent tight to opponent

Pictures

Your Notes:

Double Leg Defense

Description:	
1. MMA Stance	All elements of MMA Stance* in place
2. Hips	Bend knees to lower hips below the hips of the opponents
3. Advancing Step Front Foot	Push off the ball of the rear foot, lift the lead foot and take half step forward
4. Body	Upper body remains in MMA stance and propels ballistically towards the opponent
5. Hands	Hands reach behind and grip the back of the opponent's knees
6. Elbows	Elbows pressed tight to the outside of opponent's mid-thigh
7. Foot	Rear footsteps parallel to lead foot on the outside of opponent's leg
8. Hips	Hips are close to opponent's body as possible
9. Head	Head is above hips pressed tightly to side of torso with eye gaze pointing up and in
10. Finish	Run through opponent landing on ground with hips down and chest up with body tight to opponent tight to opponent

Pictures

 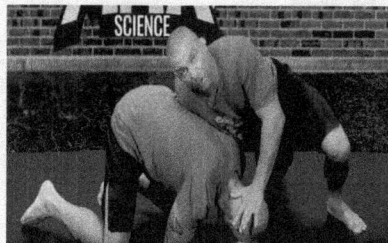 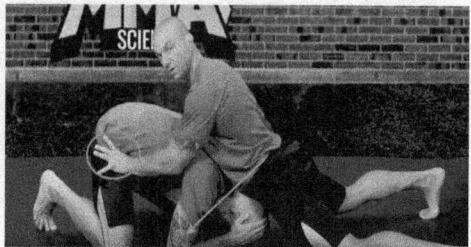

Your Notes:

Half Guard Top

Description: The Half Guard Top is a pivotal technique focuses as it is central to many areas related to offensive and defensive techniques. Pivotal techniques provide opportunities for improvement in other techniques and associated desired outcomes.

1. Knees	The leg that is not trapped is tight to the body, pinching the hip
2. Feet	Bottom of toes flat to the ground ("toes engaged")
3. Torso	Chest to chest
4. Hands	Outside hand in underhook*
5. Hands	Inside hand under head
6. Shoulder	Inside shoulder pressing tight to opponents face

Pictures

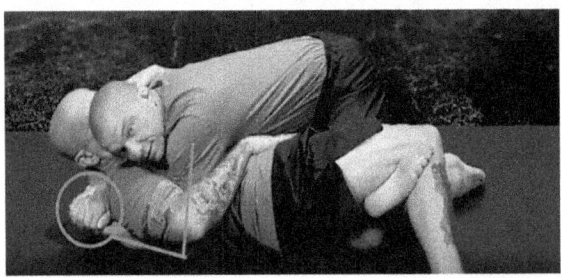 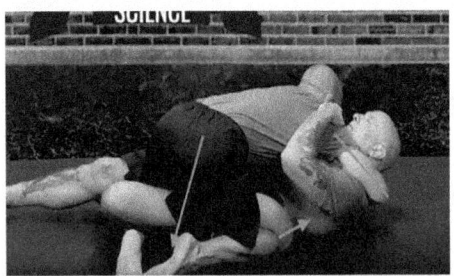

Your Notes:

Yellow Belt Skill Scoresheet

MMA Stance			Lateral Footwork			Linear Footwork		
Target	Yes	No	Target	Yes	No	Target	Yes	No
1. Rear Foot Placement			1. Lead side Step			1. Advancing Step Front Foot		
2. Front Foot Placement			2. Lead Step Back Foot			2. Advancing Step Back Foot		
3. Foot Spacing			3. Feet Spacing			3. Feet Spacing		
4. Balance			4. Rear Side Step Back Foot			4. Retreating Back Foot		
5. Knees			5. Rear Step Front Foot			5. Retreating Step Front Foot		
6. Body Orientation			6. Feet Spacing			6. Feet Spacing		
7. Back Position			7. Stance			7. Stance		
8. Elbow Position			8.			8.		
9. Hand Height			9.			9.		
10. Head Positioning			10.			10.		
Percentage Correct	%		Percentage Correct	%		Percentage Correct	%	

Your Notes:

Basic Head Movement			Jab			Parry Jab		
Target	Yes	No	Target	Yes	No	Target	Yes	No
1. Rear foot head movement			1. Stance			1. Stance		
2. Rear foot balance			2. Advancing Step Front Foot			2. Hand		
3. Rear Head Movement			3. Strike			3. Elbow		
4. Return to stance			4. Advancing Step Back Foot			4. Return		
5. Lead foot head movement			5. Feet Spacing			5.		
6. Lead foot balance			6. Retreating Back Foot			6.		
7. Lead head movement			7. Retreating Step Front Foot			7.		
8. Level change head movement			8. Feet Spacing			8.		
9. Stance			9. Stance			9.		
10.			10.			10.		
Percentage Correct	%		Percentage Correct	%		Percentage Correct	%	

Your Notes:

Cross			Block Cross			Lead Leg Front Kick		
Target	Yes	No	Target	Yes	No	Target	Yes	No
1. Stance			1. Stance			1. Stance		
2. Hips			2. Hands			2. Rear Pivot		
3. Rear Pivot			3. Torso			3. Strike		
4. Strike			4. Elbow			4. Hips		
5. Knuckles Down			5. Return			5. Upper body		
6. Stance			6.			6. Stance		
7.			7.			7.		
8.			8.			8.		
9.			9.			9.		
10.			10			10.		
Percentage Correct		%	Percentage Correct		%	Percentage Correct		%

Your Notes:

Rear Leg Front Kick			Lead Leg Front Kick Defense			Rear Leg Front Kick Defense		
Target	Yes	No	Target	Yes	No	Target	Yes	No
1. Stance			1. Stance			1. Stance		
2. Rear Pivot			2. Rear Foot			2. Lead Foot		
3. Hips			3. Upper Body			3. Upper Body		
4. Strike			4. Hips			4. Hips		
5. Lead Pivot			5. Lead Foot			5. Rear Foot		
6. Hips			6. Stance			6. Stance		
7. Hands			7.			7.		
8. Stance			8.			8.		
9.			9.			9.		
10.			10.			10.		
Percentage Correct		%	Percentage Correct		%	Percentage Correct		%

Your Notes:

YELLOW BELT

Full Guard Top			Full Guard Bottom			Basic Bridge		
Target	Yes	No	Target	Yes	No	Target	Yes	No
1. Knees			1. Legs			1. Head		
2. Feet			2. Knees			2. Torso		
3. Buttocks			3. Hands			3. Feet		
4. Posture			4. Head			4. Knees		
5. Hands			5. Shoulders			5. Hands		
6. Elbows			6.			6. Hips		
7. Head			7.			7. Return		
8.			8.			8.		
9.			9.			9.		
10.			10.			10.		
Percentage Correct		%	Percentage Correct		%	Percentage Correct		%

Your Notes:

Bridge and Reach			Bridge and Roll			Bridge and Shrimp		
Target	Yes	No	Target	Yes	No	Target	Yes	No
1. Head			1. Head			1. Head		
2. Torso			2. Torso			2. Torso		
3. Feet			3. Feet			3. Feet		
4. Knees			4. Knees			4. Knees		
5. Hands			5. Hands			5. Hands		
6. Hips			6. Hips			6. Hips		
7. Arm			7. Arm			7. Torso		
8. Return			8. Legs			8. Foot		
9.			9. Hand			9. Arms/Legs		
10.			10. Finish			10. Return		
Percentage Correct		%	Percentage Correct		%	Percentage Correct		%

Your Notes:

Technical MMA Get Up			Rear Knee			Rear Knee Defense		
Target	Yes	No	Target	Yes	No	Target	Yes	No
1. Position			1. Stance			1. Stance		
2. Bridge/shrimp			2. Rear pivot			2. Lead foot		
3. Hip*			3. Hips			3. Upper body		
4. Sit up			4. Strike			4. Rear foot		
5. Arm			5. Front pivot			5. Hips		
6. Elbow			6. Hips			6. Stance		
7. Hips			7. Upper Body			7.		
8. Foot			8. Stance			8.		
9. Head			9.			9.		
10. Finish			10.			10.		
Percentage Correct	%		Percentage Correct	%		Percentage Correct	%	

Your Notes:

Underhook			Overhook			Pummeling		
Target	Yes	No	Target	Yes	No	Target	Yes	No
1. Stance			1. Stance			1. Stance		
2. Hand			2. Grip			2. Swim hands		
3. Leg			3. Elbow			3.		
4. Grip			4. Head			4.		
5. Elbow			5. Knees			5.		
6. Head			6.			6.		
7. Knees			7.			7.		
8.			8.			8.		
9.			9.			9.		
10.			10.			10.		
Percentage Correct	%		Percentage Correct	%		Percentage Correct	%	

Your Notes:

YELLOW BELT

Body Lock			Collar Tie			Half Guard Bottom		
Target	Yes	No	Target	Yes	No	Target	Yes	No
1. Double Underhook			1. MMA Stance			1. Leg		
2. Grips			2. Arms			2. Hands		
3. Elbows			3. Forearm			3. Hips		
4. Foot			4. Elbow			4. Shoulders		
5. Hips			5. Hand			5.		
6. Knees			6.			6.		
7. Head			7.			7.		
8. Head to Chest			8.			8.		
9. Finish			9.			9.		
10.			10.			10.		
Percentage Correct		%	Percentage Correct		%	Percentage Correct		%

Your Notes:

Basic Double Leg			Half Guard Top					
Target	Yes	No	Target	Yes	No	Target	Yes	No
1. MMA Stance			1. Knees			1.		
2. Hips			2. Feet			2.		
3. Advancing Step Front Foot			3. Torso			3.		
4. Body			4. Hands			4.		
5. Hands			5. Hands			5.		
6. Elbows			6. Shoulder			6.		
7. Foot			7.			7.		
8. Hips			8.			8.		
9. Head			9.			9.		
10. Finish			10.			10.		
Percentage Correct		%	Percentage Correct		%	Percentage Correct		%

Your Notes:

Target	Yes	No	Target	Yes	No	Target	Yes	No
1.			1.			1.		
2.			2.			2.		
3.			3.			3.		
4.			4.			4.		
5.			5.			5.		
6.			6.			6.		
7.			7.			7.		
8.			8.			8.		
9.			9.			9.		
10.			10.			10.		
Percentage Correct		%	**Percentage Correct**		%	**Percentage Correct**		%

Your Notes:

YELLOW BELT

Total Performance Scorecard

	Skills Passed	Yes	No	Notes
Striking	MMA Stance			
	Jab			
	Cross			
	Straight Knee			
	Rear Leg Push kick			
	Lead Leg Push kick			
	Basic Head Movement			
	Linear Foot Work			
	Lateral Foot Work			
	Parry jab			
	Block Cross			
	Block Straight Knee			
	Block Rear Leg Push Kick			
	Block Lead Leg Push Kick			
Grappling	Underhook			
	Overhook			
	Pummeling			
	Body Lock			
	Collar Tie			
	Full Guard Top			
	Basic Double leg			
	Side Control Top			
	Basic Bridging			
	Bridge and Reach			
	Bridge and Roll			
	Bridge and Shrimp			
	Full Guard Bottom			
	Side Control Bottom			
	Tech MMA Get Up			
	Total		%	Scoring Criteria: 80%>=Pass 79%-60%=Eligible for Retest >59%=fail

Yellow Belt Criteria Met: ☐ Yes ☐ No

If no, eligible for retest? ☐ Yes ☐ No

International Mixed Martial Arts Ranking System:

ORANGE BELT

ORANGE BELT SKILLSET

	Offense and Positioning		Defense and Positioning	
Striking	**Striking Stand Up**			
	Lead hook	Lead leg round house defense	Block lead hook	Rolls
	Rear overhand	Neutral stance circling	Block step knee	
	Lead leg round-kick		Rear leg round house defense	
	Rear leg round-kick			
	Striking Clinch			
	Body lock defense			
	Striking Ground			
	Elbows in full guard			
	Hammer fist in full guard			
Grappling	Side Control – Top	Head inside single defense	Side Control - Bottom	Scissor sweep
	Arm bar from the mount	Head inside single	MMA technical stand up-full guard	Sprawl-whizzer
	Basic mid mount	Head outside single defense	Replace guard from half guard	
	Full guard bottom bicep ride	Head outside single	Replace guard from side control	
	Posture guard pass	Hitchhiker escape		
	Knee on belly	Knee shield		

Block Lead Hook

Description: Blocking the lead hook is a high frequency and critical behaviors as hooks are punches that are routinely thrown. While the Lead Hook Block is intended as a defense, when done correctly it also sets up offense as the slight rotation of the torso "loads" an offensive technique. For example, if a right handed fighter throws a lead hook at another right handed fighter, the defending fighter might absorb the hook by rotating their torso slightly to the left which then simultaneously "loads" their own hook.

1. Stance	All elements of MMA stance in place
2. Hands	Using an open or closed fist, slightly raise the hand and secure it to the head near the temple
3. Torso	Rotate torso slightly in the same direction the punch is moving to absorb the hook
4. Elbow	Elbow remains pointed towards the ground and close to body
5. Return	Return to MMA Stance

Pictures

Your Notes:

Rear Leg Roundhouse Defense

Description: A low frequency technique the Rear Leg Roundhouse can be a devastating strike. It is important that the fighter avoid "reaching" for the kick and ensure a strong MMA stance as the body mechanics of the strike can be mistaken for a leg or body kick. Fighters who lower their guard anticipating either of these strikes risk receiving the impact of this extremely powerful strike.

1. Stance	All elements of MMA stance in place
2. Hands -1	Using an open or closed fist, slightly raise the hand and secure it to the head near the temple.
3. Hands - 2	Using an open hand, the opposite hand extends at approximately 45 degrees towards the kick
4. Torso	Rotate torso slightly in the same direction kick is moving while simultaneously using the extended hand to absorb the round house
5. Elbow	Elbow remains pointed towards the ground and close to body
6. Return	Return to MMA Stance

Pictures

Your Notes:

Bottom – Guard Replace

Description: This is important technique as side control top provides the opponent many offensive options while providing very limited options to the fighter being controlled. In side control bottom position, it is critical the fighter avoid being flat on their back to provide escape other positioning options.

1. Shrimp	Use shrimping* technique to face opponent
2. Torso	Turn torso slightly towards opponent by elevating hip
3. Feet	Bottom of feet flat on the ground pulled close to buttocks
4. Knees	Pointed up
5. Hands	Elbows tight to body, palms facing each other
6. Hips	Ballistically elevate hips vertically
7. Torso	Rotate torso down to either side until the shoulder and foot on that side are the only areas of the body touching the ground
8. Foot	Keep foot planted on the ground and move hips away from feet
9. Arms/Legs	Arms and legs are fully extended
10. Return	Return to basic bridge position

Pictures

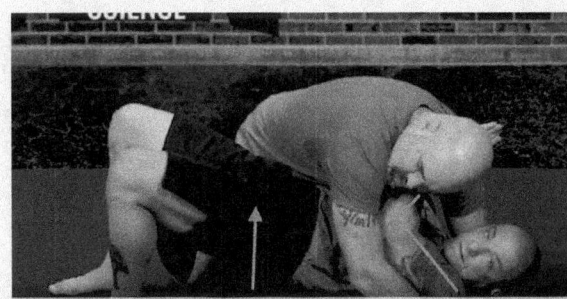 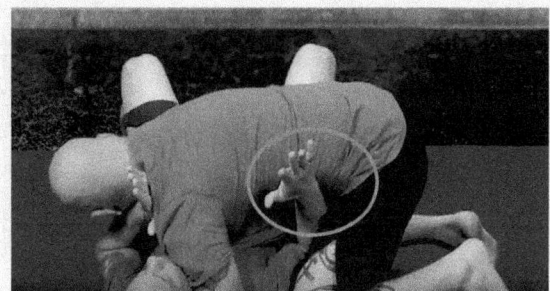

Your Notes:

Rear Overhand

Description: In MMA, the rear overhand is can be a devastating punch when accurate and thrown under the right conditions. Great care must be used when throwing the overhand as it tends to open the fighter up for a counter. For example, a straight punch delivered simultaneously by an opponent is likely to land first. Moving the head off line is extremely important for generating power and acting as a defensive "slip" to avoid counters. The angle of the overhand as well as the bend of the elbow can be tactically adjusted based on elements like distance and height.

1. Stance	All elements of MMA stance in place
2. Hips	Rotate to hips forward to a 90 degree angle
3. Rear Pivot	Pivot the rear foot from 45 to a 90 degree angle and shift weight to lead foot
4. Strike	Propel the rear hand from the cheek ballistically forward in a 45 degree angle with in a lead hand held at temple
5. Head	Head moves slightly forward and off line at approximately 45 degrees
6. Elbow	Elbow remains bent at approximately 90 degrees
7. Knuckles Down	The knuckles should face toward fighter
8. Stance	Return to MMA stance

Pictures

Your Notes:

Rolls

Description: The roll is a fundamental movement used to avoid hooks and overhands. In MMA, rolling can be risky as it exposes the fighter to kicks and knees. As such, it is critical that posture with a high guard be maintained throughout the entire defensive movement.

1. Stance	Beginning from the MMA Stance
2. Rear foot head movement	Trunk rotates towards the rear foot
3. Rear foot balance	Balance shifts towards the rear foot
4. Level change rear head Movement	As trunk and balance shift, head is simultaneously lowered below arch of incoming hook using a slight bending of the knees below chest level. All elements of the MMA Stance are maintained.
5. Return to stance	Trunk and head return to MMA stance
6. Lead foot head movement	Trunk rotates towards the lead foot
7. Lead foot balance	Balance shifts towards the lead foot
8. Lead change forward head movement	As trunk and balance shift, head is simultaneously lowered below arch of incoming hook or overhand using a slight bending of the knees. All elements of the MMA Stance are maintained.
9. Level change head movement	Bend knees, head lowers below chest level
10. Stance	All elements of stance maintained

Pictures

Your Notes:

Lead Hook

Description: The hook is a power punch that can be devastating when set up with a slip or thrown as the opponent moves laterally towards the fighter's lead hook. Where the cross is thrown ballistically forward and can be done so from the MMA Stance, the hook is more of a swinging punch and often requires the fighter to position himself/herself appropriately or move the opponent into the appropriate position.

1. Stance	All elements of MMA stance in place
2. Hips and Trunk	Rotate hips forward to a 90 degree angle
3. Rear Pivot	Pivot the rear foot from 45 to a 90 degree angle and shift weight to lead foot
4. Strike	Propel lead hand from the cheek ballistically in an arching motion forward in a 45 degree angle with in a lead hand held at temple
5. Hips and Trunk	Shift hips from backwards to just beyond the MMA stance positioning
6. Lead Pivot	Lead foot pivots slightly to the inside in the direction of the punch
7. Head	Head moves slightly backwards
8. Elbow	Elbow remains bent at approximately 90 degrees
9. Knuckles Down	The knuckles should face toward fighter
10. Stance	Return to MMA stance

Pictures

Your Notes:

ORANGE BELT

Lead Leg Kick

Description: Kicks are extremely dangerous strikes that can be focused anywhere on the legs, torso, and head. All kicks start on the same line of attack with the goal of hitting the target with the lower portion of the shin.

1. Stance	All elements of the MMA stance in place
2. Rear foot	Rear foot steps forward at approximately a 45 degree angle
3. Head	Off center line
4. Lead hand	Lead hand frame with chin behind shoulder
5. Rear foot	Push off the ball of the rear foot
6. Hip	Drive hip forward
7. Balance	Weight transfers to front foot
8. Knee	Moves ballistically in a straight line
9. Hip	Hip swings lead leg to rotate through target with foot in dorsiflexion
10. Rear foot	Rear foot continues to rotate until heal is pointed at targeted

Pictures

Your Notes:

Rear leg round kick

Description: This is one of the most powerful strikes in the mixed martial artists arsenal. It can be focused at the leg, torso, and head.

1. Stance	All elements of the MMA Stance in place
2. Lead foot	Lead foot steps forward at approximately a 45 degree angle
3. Head	Off center line
4. Rear hand	Rear hand frame with chin behind shoulder
5. Rear foot	Push off the ball of the rear foot
6. Hip	Drive hip forward
7. Balance	Weight transfers to front foot
8. Knee	Moves ballistically in a straight line
9. Hip	Hip swings rear leg to rotate through target with foot in dorsiflexion
10. Lead foot	Lead foot continues to rotate until heal is pointed at targeted

Pictures

Your Notes:

Lead Leg Roundhouse Defense

Description: A low frequency technique the Lead Leg Roundhouse Defense can be a devastating strike. It is important that the fighter avoid "reaching" for the kick and ensure a strong MMA stance as the body mechanics of the strike can be mistaken for a leg or body kick. Fighters who lower their guard anticipating either of these strikes risk receiving the impact of this extremely powerful strike.

1. Stance	All elements of MMA stance in place
2. Hands -1	Using an open or closed fist, slightly raise the hand and secure it to the head near the temple.
3. Hands - 2	Using an open hand, the opposite hand extends at approximately 45 degrees towards the kick
4. Torso	Rotate torso slightly in the same direction kick is moving while simultaneously using the extended hand to absorb the round house
5. Elbow	Elbow remains pointed towards the ground and close to body
6. Return	Return to MMA Stance

Pictures

Your Notes:

Neutral stance circling

Description: Footwork is one of the most important aspects of MMA as it allows the martial artist to remain in a position to initiate offense or defend the opponent's offense.

1. Stance	All elements of MMA stance in place.
2. Lead Side Step	Push off the ball of the rear foot, lift the lead foot and take half step laterally
3. Lead Step Back Foot	Rear foot follows and moves equal distance sideways
4. Rear hand	Rear hand frame with chin behind shoulder
5. Lead foot	Pivot on the lead foot and return to MMA Stance
6.	
7. Rear Side Step Back Foot	Push off the ball of the lead foot, lift the rear foot and take half step laterally
8. Rear Step Front Foot	Lead foot follows and moves equal distance sideways
9. Rear hand	Rear hand frame with chin behind shoulder
10. Lead foot	Lead foot steps forward and return to MMA Stance

Pictures

Your Notes:

Body lock defense

Description: A body lock is a hold in which the arms are locked tightly round an opponent's chest and arms and is often used to take an opponent down. The body lock defense is intended to put the martial in a neutral position.

1. Stance	Beginning from a standing position, the opponent has the body lock secured
2. Hands	Each palm is simultaneously placed on the opponents to hips to maintain separation
3. Whizzer	Using either hand, turn whizzer down to create shoulder pressure
4. Foot	Step opposite foot back to create space
5. Hands	Pummel under hook on the same side of the foot that is stepped back to enter into neutral position

Pictures

Your Notes:

Elbows in Full Guard

Description: Elbows from the full guard are a dangerous technique that can cut and even render an opponent unconscious. A key to getting the most out of elbows is to keep the hand open to expose the blade of the elbow.

1. Full guard top	Begin from the full guard top position
2. Torso	Rotate the torso to generate power
3. Elbow	Roll elbow 45 degree angle towards the target.
4. Hands	Striking elbow hand remains open
5. Full guard top	Return to full guard top position

Pictures

 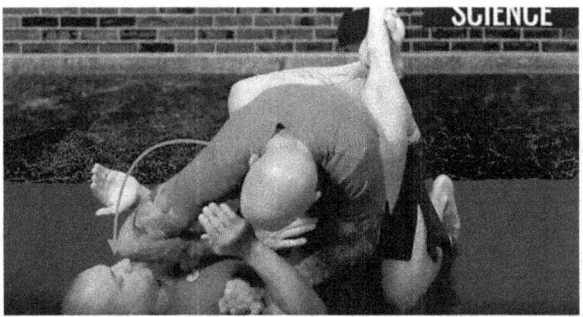

Your Notes:

Hammer fist in full guard

Description: Commonly used during ground striking, The hammerfist use movement similar to swinging a hammer to deliver a strike is a strike with side of a clenched fist, using an action like swinging a hammer, but can also be used horizontally like a back. A key to the hammer fist is to keep the arm relaxed and the elbow in line with the target

1. Full guard top	Begin from the full guard top position
2. Torso	Posture up
3. Hand	Ballistically drive closed fist towards target
4. Elbow	Striking elbow remains close to body
5. Full guard top	Return to full guard top position

Pictures

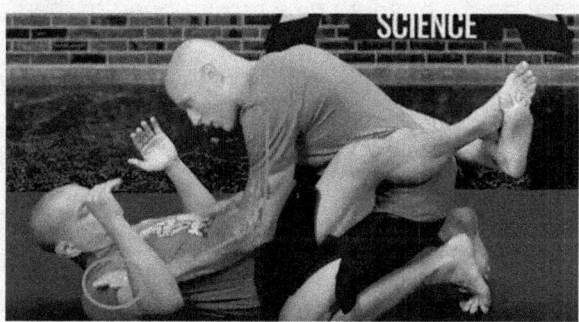 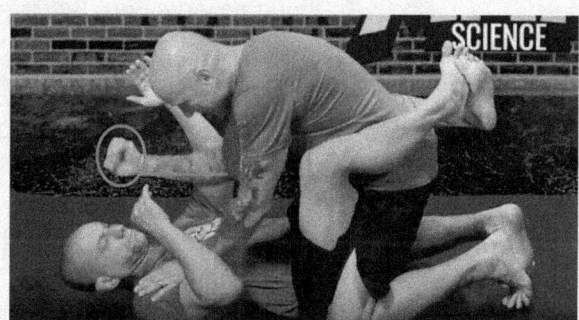

Your Notes:

Arm bar from the mount	
Description: Arm bars are a high frequency submission technique in MMA and can be very effective from a high mount. It is important the martial artist use strikes to set up the arm bar mount.	
1. Full mount	Begin from a full mount position.
2. Hands	Hands remain on shoulders
3. Knees	Knees slide into the arm pits
4. Hands (options)	Option 1: Both hands can either be on the center of the chest Option 2: One hand on the chest, one hand on the face and push it away
5. Knee	Slide the knee up on the side of the arm being attacked
6. Leg	Turn instep of foot towards the ceiling with heal as close to ear as possible
7. Balance	Transfer weight over the attacking arm towards the opposite knee
8. Leg	Simultaneously put leg over the opponent's head as hips are dropped to the floor and tight to the opponent
9. Knees/Grips	Pinch knees together, heels pointed towards the mat. Release underhook and grip wrists with both hands
10. Hips	Use the fulcrum of hip on side of crotch further away from the opponent's head and drive hips to the ceiling.

Pictures

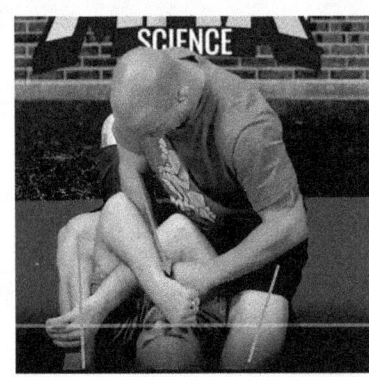

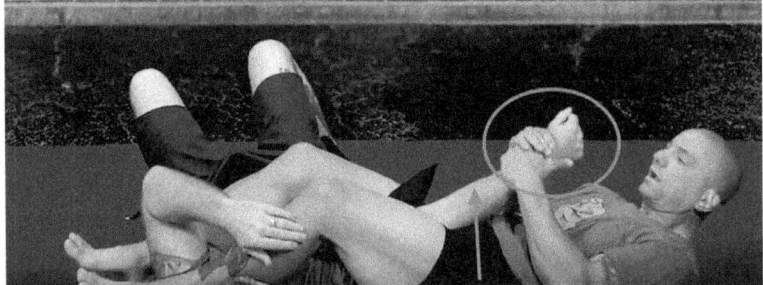

Basic Mid Mount

Description: Mid mount allows the martial to control the opponent and strike when needed. It also allows the martial artist to move from low mount to high mount as needed.

1. Mount	Begin in a position with knees mid torso
2. Hips	Hips are pressed tight to opponent's mid-torso.
3. Hands	Palms facing down flat on the mat just beyond shoulders width, approximately just above the opponent's torso
4. Knees	Knees are pinched tight to torso

Pictures

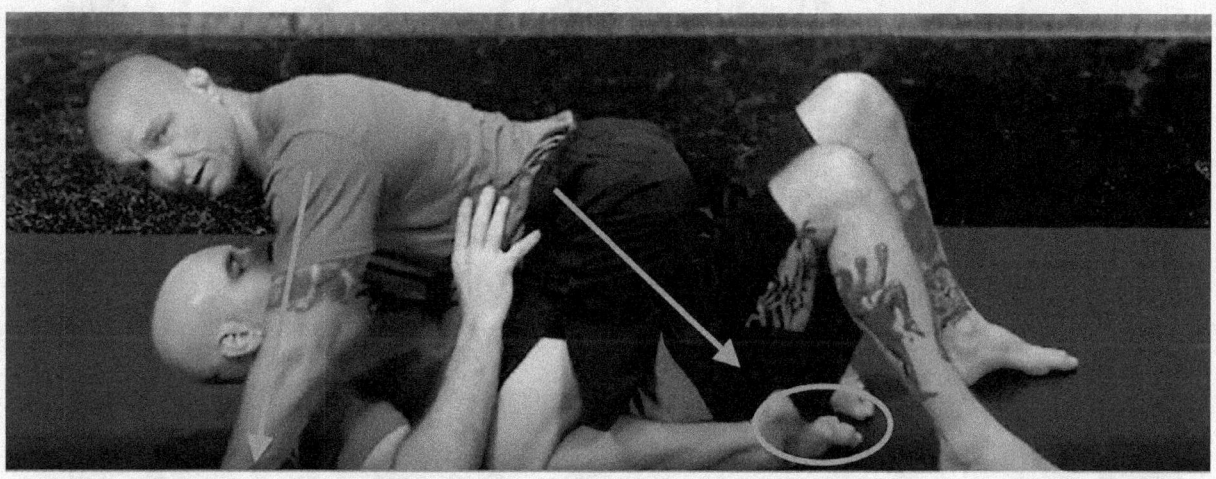

Your Notes:

Full Guard Bottom Bicep Ride

Description: Full guard bottom bicep ride is an effective defensive technique that allows the martial artist to avoid strikes and set up a technical get up. The key to this is winning the inside position through effective pummeling.

1. Guard	Begin from the full guard bottom
2. Pummel	Pummel arms to the inside
3. Hands	Put palms on each bicep

Pictures

Your Notes:

Posture Guard Pass

Description: When scoring a takedown or landing in the opponent's guard for any reason, it's often better to improve position for striking and submissions. The key here is to use striking to set up the pass.

1. Position	Begin from the full guard top
2. Hands	Pin the opponent's forearm across their belly with hands
3. Leg	Post leg on the side of the arm that is trapped
4. Knees	Pinch knee of the posted foot tight to opponent's body
5. Leg	Post the other leg with knees pinching the opponent's legs
6. Hip	Drive hips forward
7. Hands	Reach back and swim opponents leg that is on the side of the trapped arm to the front
8. Side control	Slide down opponent's leg and establish side control

Pictures

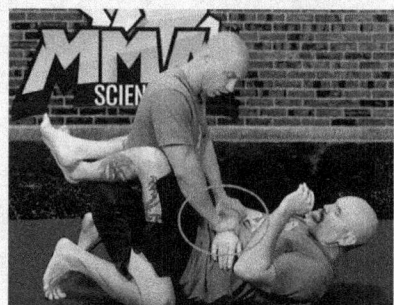 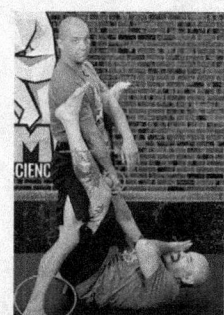 

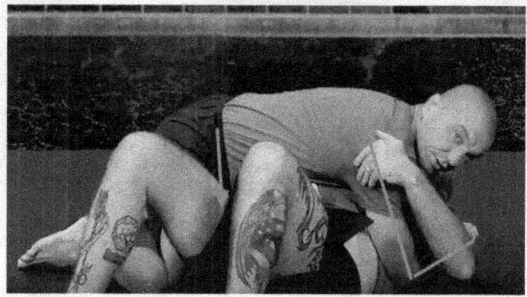

Your Notes:

Knee on Belly

Description: A dominant position where the martial artist places a knee on opponents' belly or different parts of the torso while maintain balance with the opposite leg extended. Not as stable as the mount, the position does allow for striking and transition into various holds, other positions, and quick disengagement when required. The key here is leveraging the head and rear foot to drive the knee into the chest to maximize pressure.

1. Knee	Put knee directly into center of chest
2. Lead foot	Foot in hip with leg tight to torso
3. Rear foot	On ball of foot driving weight towards knee
4. Lead hand	Collar tie head and pull forward off the mat
5. Rear hand	Placed on hip driving it down

Pictures

Your Notes:

Head Outside Single Leg Takedown Defense

Description: Single leg takedowns are one of the most common takedowns in MMA and can leave the martial artist in a poor position if unable to defend. Because of the high frequency of this takedown, it is critical to for the martial artist to develop strong takedown defense. Key to this takedown defense is remaining square to the opponent.

1. Position	Opponent has head outside single
2. Legs	Lower level by bending legs
3. Lead hand	As level changes, simultaneously use cross face to push opponent's head to the inside
4. Whizzer	Use whizzer to escape
5. Rear hand	Pummel in with free hand to under over position

Pictures

 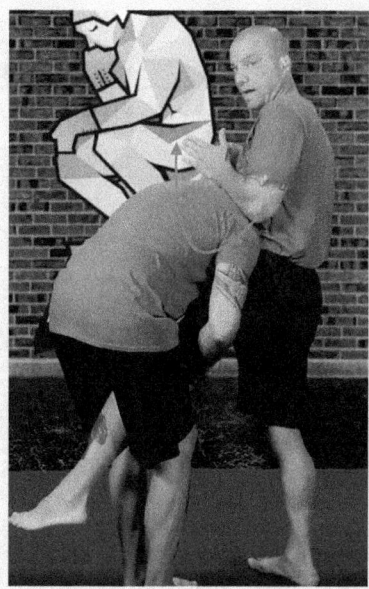

Your Notes:

Head Inside Single Leg Takedown

Description: The single leg takedown involves the martial artist grabbing one of the legs of the opponent, typically with both hands, and bringing the opponent to the ground using leverage and force as the lower part of the leg is pulled in one direction while the shoulder or torso are used to drive the upper part of the leg or body in the opposite direction. A frequent key to takedowns is using strikes to set them up.

1. Stance	All elements of the MMA Stance in place
2. Footwork	Linear footwork to penetrate forward using entry strike
3. Rear foot	Step foot to the outside of the opponents leg
4. Lead hand	Hook lead hand tightly to opponent's crotch through the rear
5. Rear hand	Hook rear hand tightly to opponent's crotch through from the front
6. Head	Facing forward, head drives directly forward with forehead into chest
7. Grips	Use grips to elevate leg with elbows tight to the body
8. Knees	Pinch knees to control leg
9. Shoulder	Use head and shoulder pressure to generate forward motion
10. Footwork	Use footwork to make a "C" motion to drive the opponent to the ground

Pictures

Your Notes:

Head Inside Single Leg Defense

Description: Single leg takedowns are one of the most common takedowns in MMA and can leave the martial artist in a poor position if unable to defend. Because of the high frequency of this takedown, it is critical to for the martial artist to develop strong takedown defense. Key to this takedown defense is remaining square to the opponent.

1. Position	Opponent has head in a head inside single.
2. Outside arm	Overhook
3. Leg	Transition leg from inside the opponent's legs to outside
4. Knee	Knee and shin are framed across the opponent's waist and used to create space
5. Free hand	Grip elbow and pull overhook forward
6. Overhook	As gripped elbow is pulled forward, simultaneously turn over hook over down
7. Foot	As overhook is turned over, simultaneously stomp foot to the floor
8. Pummel	Pummel to 50/50 position

Pictures

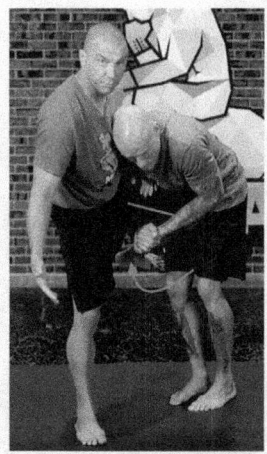

Your Notes:

Head Outside Single Leg Takedown

Description: Single leg takedowns are one of the most common takedowns in MMA and can leave the martial artist in a poor position if unable to defend. Because of the high frequency of this takedown, it is critical to for the martial artist to develop strong takedown defense. Key to this takedown defense is remaining square to the opponent.

1. Stance	All elements of the MMA Stance in place
2. Footwork	Linear footwork to penetrate forward using entry strike
3. Knees	Bend knees to change levels
4. Hands	Both hands "snake" behind opponent's knees
5. Head	Pressed tight to the torso below the opponent's armpit
6. Rear leg	Positioned forward parallel to the leg
7. Arms	Pull opponents legs tightly to the body
8. Shoulder	Turn inside shoulder pressure into the opponent's hip to shift the weigh to the opponents back leg
9. Outside leg	Step straight back with the outside leg
10. Body	Turn body and bow to the mat to propel the opponent to the ground

Pictures

Your Notes:

Hitchhiker Escape

Description: Arm bars are one of the highest percentage submissions attempt and completed in MMA today. Typically used as a last resort, one of the easiest to implement yet most important escapes the martial artist can learn for escaping armbars is the hitchhiker escape which is as simple as turning the thumb down to prevent the opponent from leveraging the elbow joint to submission. A common mistake when performing this technique that is when the martial artists turns their hips towards the opponent instead of away.

1. Position	Beginning from prone position trapped in opponents arm bar with thumb up
2. Arm	Turn thumb down towards opponent by rotating arm
3. Hips	Bridge and roll
4. Feet	Walk hits in a circular motion until arm is no longer in submission
5. Hands	Control leg with inside hand
6. Movement	Walk up the side of the leg with head outside of guard and ear pressured tight to opponent's body
7. Side control	Finish in side control

Pictures

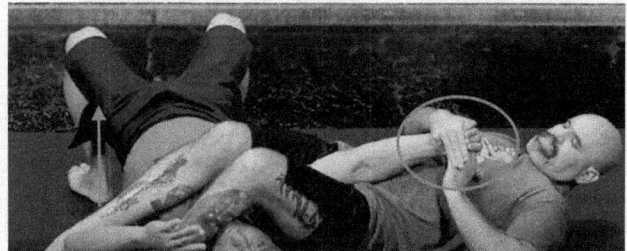
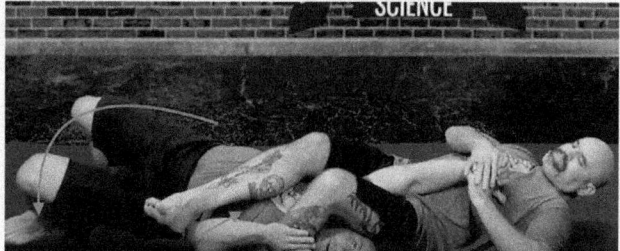

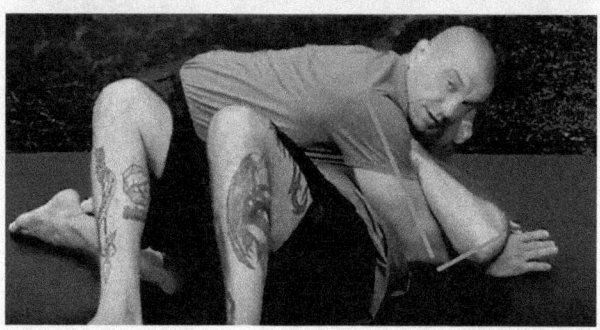

Your Notes:

Knee Shield

Description: A properly placed knee shield is a simple technique for keeping the opponent's weight off of the martial artist while controlling distance to prevent strikes or set up transitions, sweeps, or escapes.

1. Position	Beginning with opponent inside full guard trolling biceps
2. Legs	Open guard with knees pinched to torso, feet flat to the ground.
3. Hips	Bridge and shrimp
4. Knee	Slide knee to center of chest facing opponent's armpit with knee and hip at approximately 90 degree angle
5. Leg	Extend leg with knee in torso to create space
6. Hands	Control biceps with hands or frame across shoulder

Pictures

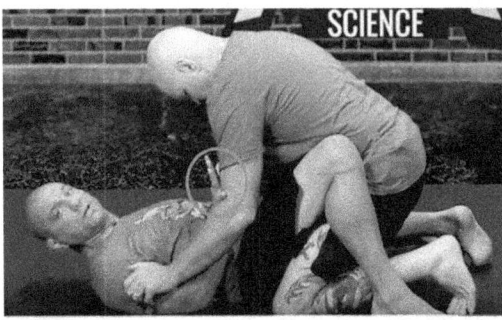
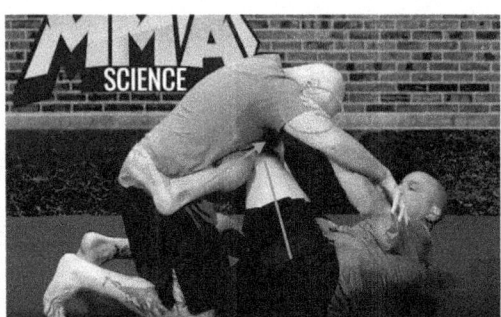
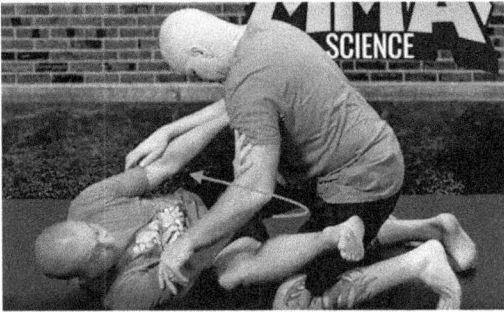

Your Notes:

ORANGE BELT

Block Lead Hook				Rear Leg Roundhouse Defense				Side Control Bottom – Guard Replace		
Target	Yes	No		Target	Yes	No		Target	Yes	No
1. Stance				1. Stance				1. Shrimp		
2. Hands				2. Hands -1				2. Torso		
3. Torso				3. Hands - 2				3. Feet		
4. Elbow				4. Torso				4. Knees		
5. Return				5. Elbow				5. Hands		
6.				6. Return				6. Hips		
7.				7.				7. Torso		
8.				8.				8. Foot		
9.				9.				9. Arms/Legs		
10.				10.				10. Return		
Percentage Correct		%		Percentage Correct		%		Percentage Correct		%

Your Notes:

Side Control Bottom – Guard Replace				Rear Overhand				Lead Hook		
Target	Yes	No		Target	Yes	No		Target	Yes	No
1. Shrimp				1. Stance				1. Stance		
2. Torso				2. Hips				2. Hips and Trunk		
3. Feet				3. Rear Pivot				3. Rear Pivot		
4. Knees				4. Strike				4. Strike		
5. Hands				5. Head				5. Hips and Trunk		
6. Hips				6. Elbow				6. Lead Pivot		
7. Torso				7. Knuckles Down				7. Head		
8. Foot				8. Stance				8. Elbow		
9. Arms/Legs				9.				9. Knuckles Down		
10. Return				10.				10. Stance		
Percentage Correct		%		Percentage Correct		%		Percentage Correct		%

Your Notes:

Rolls			Lead Leg Kick			Rear leg round kick		
Target	Yes	No	Target	Yes	No	Target	Yes	No
1. Stance			1. Stance			1. Stance		
Rear foot head movement			2. Rear foot			2. Lead foot		
3. Rear foot balance			3. Head			3. Head		
4. Level change rear head Movement			4. Lead hand			4. Rear hand		
5. Return to stance			5. Rear foot			5. Rear foot		
6. Lead foot head movement			6. Hip			6. Hip		
7. Lead foot balance			7. Balance			7. Balance		
8. Lead change forward head movement			8. Knee			8. Knee		
9. Level change head movement			9. Hip			9. Hip		
10. Stance			10. Rear foot			10. Lead foot		
Percentage Correct		%	Percentage Correct		%	Percentage Correct		%

Your Notes:

Lead Leg Roundhouse Defense			Neutral stance circling			Body lock defense		
Target	Yes	No	Target	Yes	No	Target	Yes	No
1. Stance			1. Stance			1. Stance		
2. Hands -1			2. Lead Side Step			2. Hands		
3. Hands - 2			3. Lead Step Back Foot			3. Whizzer		
4. Torso			4. Rear hand			4. Foot		
5. Elbow			5. Lead foot			5. Hands		
6. Return			6.			6.		
7.			7. Rear Side Step Back Foot			7.		
8.			8. Rear Step Front Foot			8.		
9.			9. Rear hand			9.		
10.			10. Lead foot			10.		
Percentage Correct		%	Percentage Correct		%	Percentage Correct		%

Your Notes:

ORANGE BELT

Elbows in Full Guard			Hammer fist in full guard			Arm bar from the mount		
Target	Yes	No	Target	Yes	No	Target	Yes	No
1. Full guard top			1. Full guard top			1. Full mount		
2. Torso			2. Torso			2. Hands		
3. Elbow			3. Hand			3. Knees		
4. Hands			4. Elbow			4. Hands (options)		
5. Full guard top			5. Full guard top			5. Knee		
6.			6.			6. Leg		
7.			7.			7. Balance		
8.			8.			8. Leg		
9.			9.			9. Knees/Grips		
10.			10.			10. Hips		
Percentage Correct		%	Percentage Correct		%	Percentage Correct		%

Your Notes:

Basic Mid Mount			Full Guard Bottom Bicep Ride			Posture Guard Pass		
Target	Yes	No	Target	Yes	No	Target	Yes	No
1. Mount			1. Guard			1. Position		
2. Hips			2. Pummel			2. Hands		
3. Hands			3. Hands			3. Leg		
4. Knees			4.			4. Knees		
5.			5.			5. Leg		
6.			6.			6. Hip		
7.			7.			7. Hands		
8.			8.			8. Side control		
9.			9.			9.		
10.			10.			10.		
Percentage Correct		%	Percentage Correct		%	Percentage Correct		%

Your Notes:

Knee on Belly			Head Outside Single Leg Takedown Defense			Head Inside Single Leg Takedown		
Target	Yes	No	Target	Yes	No	Target	Yes	No
1. Knee			1. Position			1. Stance		
2. Lead foot			2. Legs			2. Footwork		
3. Rear foot			3. Lead hand			3. Rear foot		
4. Lead hand			4. Whizzer			4. Lead hand		
5. Rear hand			5. Rear hand			5. Rear hand		
6.			6.			6. Head		
7.			7.			7. Grips		
8.			8.			8. Knees		
9.			9.			9. Shoulder		
10.			10.			10. Footwork		
Percentage Correct		%	Percentage Correct		%	Percentage Correct		%

Your Notes:

Head Inside Single Leg Takedown			Head Inside Single Leg Defense			Head Outside Single Leg Takedown		
Target	Yes	No	Target	Yes	No	Target	Yes	No
1. Stance			1. Position			1. Stance		
2. Footwork			2. Outside arm			2. Footwork		
3. Rear foot			3. Leg			3. Knees		
4. Lead hand			4. Knee			4. Hands		
5. Rear hand			5. Free hand			5. Head		
6. Head			6. Overhook			6. Rear leg		
7. Grips			7. Foot			7. Arms		
8. Knees			8. Pummel			8. Shoulder		
9. Shoulder			9.			9. Outside leg		
10. Footwork			10.			10. Body		
Percentage Correct		%	Percentage Correct		%	Percentage Correct		%

Your Notes:

ORANGE BELT

Hitchhiker Escape			Knee Shield					
Target	**Yes**	**No**	**Target**	**Yes**	**No**	**Target**	**Yes**	**No**
1. Position			1. Position			1.		
2. Arm			2. Legs			2.		
3. Hips			3. Hips			3.		
4. Feet			4. Knee			4.		
5. Hands			5. Leg			5.		
6. Movement			6. Hands			6.		
7. Side control			7.			7.		
8.			8.			8.		
9.			9.			9.		
10.			10.			10.		
Percentage Correct		%	**Percentage Correct**		%	**Percentage Correct**		%

Your Notes:

Target	**Yes**	**No**	**Target**	**Yes**	**No**	**Target**	**Yes**	**No**
Percentage Correct		%	**Percentage Correct**		%	**Percentage Correct**		%

Your Notes:

	Total Performance Scorecard			
	Skills Passed	Yes	No	Notes
Striking	MMA Stance			
	Jab			
	Cross			
	Straight Knee			
	Rear Leg Push kick			
	Lead Leg Push kick			
	Basic Head Movement			
	Linear Foot Work			
	Lateral Foot Work			
	Parry jab			
	Block Cross			
	Block Straight Knee			
	Block Rear Leg Push Kick			
	Block Lead Leg Push Kick			
Grappling	Underhook			
	Overhook			
	Pummeling			
	Double Underhook			
	Body Lock			
	Collar Tie			
	Full Guard Top			
	Basic Double leg			
	Side Control Top			
	Basic Bridging			
	Bridge and Reach			
	Bridge and Roll			
	Bridge and Shrimp			
	Full Guard Bottom			
	Side Control Bottom			
	Tech MMA Get Up			
	Total		%	Scoring Criteria: 80%>=Pass 79%-60%=Eligible for Retest >59%=fail

Orange Belt Criteria Met: ☐ Yes ☐ No

If no, eligible for retest? ☐ Yes ☐ No

International Mixed Martial Arts Ranking System:
GREEN BELT

Green Belt Skillset

	Offense and Positioning		Defense and Positioning	
Striking	45_Step	Pivoting	Switch Snap	Inside low kick defense
	Inside low kick	Rear uppercut	Switch step	Rear uppercut defense
	Lead uppercut	Switch Round house kick		Lead uppercut defense
	Outside low kick	Switch knee		Outside low kick defense
Grappling	Back mount position	Front head lock	Guillotine from the guard defense	
	Guillotine from the guard	MMA Clinch	Mount Escape	
	Inside trip	Outside trip	Rear naked choke defense	
	Rear naked choke	Snap down		
	Standing guillotine			

45 Step

Description: The 45 degree step allows the martial artist to avoid the opponent's office to set up a counter offensive technique like a strike or takedown.

1. Stance	All elements of MMA Stance in place
2. Hands	Strike with the jab cross
3. Rear Foot	Rear footsteps approximately 45 degree angle and lead foot
4. Lead Foot	Steps approximately the same distance
5. Positioning	Body positioned just outside of the opponents lead shoulder
6. Stance	All elements of MMA stance in place

Pictures

Your Notes:

Back Mount Position

Description: A rear naked choke is one of the highest percentage submissions in MMA. Before that can be finished, it is critical for the martial artist to understand the fundamental position of the back mount. The two major components of this position are hooks and the seat belt to counter or control the opponent's movement.

1. Position	Begin on opponents back with hooks in
2. Feet	Feet on Inside of thighs, toes flexed (do not cross feet)
3. Arms	One arm extended forward under the opponents arm bit, the other over the opponents opposite shoulder.
4. Hands	The hand extended under the opponent's arm is placed as the top, thumb less grip
5. Positioning	Pull opponent close to chest.
6. Head	Pressed tightly to opponent's head, ear next to opponents' ear.

Pictures

  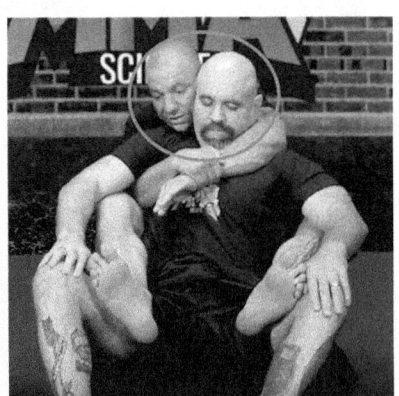

Your Notes:

Front Head Lock Positioning

Description: The front head lock can be entered from many different approaches to control the opponents aggression.

1. Position	Begin with opponent's head pressed to side of torso
2. Inside Arm	Overhooks head
3. Lead Hand	With open palm "cups" chin
4. Elbow	Pressed tightly to opponent's ear
5. Rear hand	Either on opponents tricep or in an underhook position

Pictures

Your Notes:

Guillotine from the Guard Defense

Description: This common submission can occur from different positions. It is important the martial artist use hand to press hip to the side and drive shoulder into opponent's chest.

1. Position	Begin in guillotine inside the opponent's guard
2. Hips	Post both feet on ground and raise hips up and forward
3. Shoulder	Press inside shoulder into the opponent's chest
4. Hand	Use inside hand to push hips towards the side the head is trapped
5. Head	Drive head towards and look towards armpit
6. Hand	Use outside hand to push opponent's elbow off head
7. Position	Finish postured up inside the opponent's full guard

Pictures

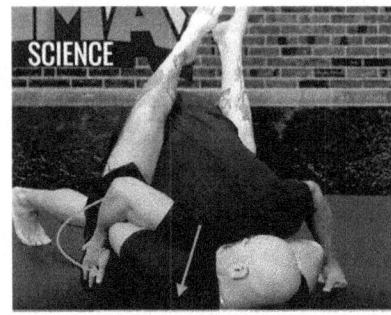  

Your Notes:

Guillotine from the Guard

Description: Guillotine is a frequently applied submission. It is important the martial artist punches their hand through the front head lock position so that the side of the wrist is under the opponent's chin approximately thumb deep.

1. Position	Begin with opponent in full guard
2. Legs	Use legs to pull opponent forward
3. Hand	Punch hand through the front headlock position so that the side of the wrist is underneath the opponent's chin
4. Grips	No thumb grip with two middle fingers on the bone of the wrist of the arm that is punched through the headlock
5. Elbows	Pull opponent close by pulling both elbows in tight to body
6. Chest	Push chest and chin tight to the opponent's body
7. Torso	Turn torso toward side ("side crunch motion") as if attempting to touch elbow to hip
8. Elbow	Choke arm with elbow should be touching or as close to the ground as possible

Pictures

 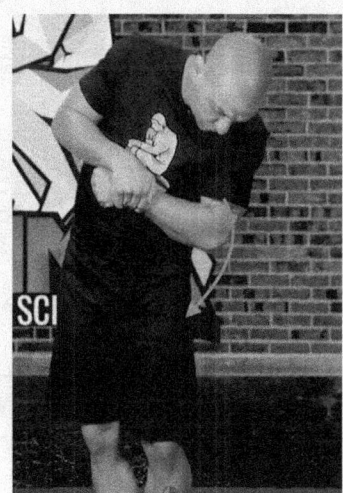 

Your Notes:

Inside Low Kick Defense

Description: Leg kicks left unchecked can render the martial artist helpless on their feet. The trick to this simple move is refrain from over rotating the knee inwards. Over rotation can result in the leg acting as a "ramp" that leads directly to the martial artist's groin.

1. Stance	All elements of MMA Stance in place
2. Lead foot	Turn foot in pivoting on the ball of the lead foot approximately 45 degrees towards incoming strike
3. Knee	As lead foot pivots on ball of foot, knee drives slightly forward
4. Knee variation	Lift knee and turn in approximately 45 degrees towards incoming strike
5. Foot	Toes curled up, small step forward

Pictures

Your Notes:

Inside Low Kick

Description: This kick is a high frequency low risk strike with moderate damage that when accrued can do great damage to the opponent. It can also be used as a set up for other offensive techniques.

1. Stance	All elements of the MMA Stance in place
2. Switch Stance	Use switch stance to load kick
3. Hand	Rear hand frames
4. Rear Foot	Pushing off the ball of the rear foot shift weight to front foot
5. Knee	Drive knee forward and up
6. Hips	Swing hips approximately 160 degrees
7. Lead foot	Pivots with hip motion approximately 160 degrees

Pictures

Your Notes:

Inside Trip

Description: Inside leg trip is a high percentage take down in MMA. It is important use the overhook and outside leg to drive forward with momentum to drive the opponent to the ground.

1. Position	Begin from the over-under position
2. Underhook	Pull the opponent forward with the underhook
3. Leg	Step the underhook leg back
4. Rear foot	Bring rear foot together with lead foot
5. Lead foot	Bring lead leg forward and step it deep between the opponent's legs and outside their foot
6. Hips	Tight to the opponents
7. Lead foot	Ball of lead foot is on the ground
8. Knee	Knee and hip drive towards the ground
9. Hooks	Pull the overhooked arm toward the ground, push the underhook up to displace the opponent's balance as chest pushes forward driving opponent to the ground
10. Position	Finish in the opponent's guard

Pictures

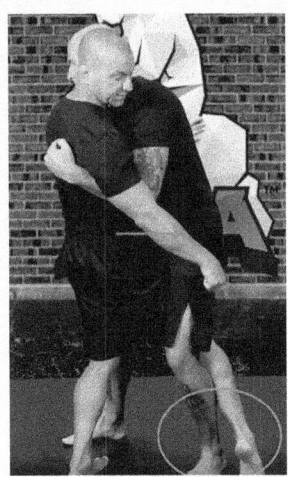  

Your Notes:

Lead Upper Cut Defense

Description: The upper cut is a component skill and a dangerous strike that is most effectively used in close proximity to the opponent. Because of the proximity required to throw an uppercut, an added safety measure is throwing it as a counter.

1. Stance	All elements of the MMA Stance in place
2. Hands	Using a fist or open palm, pull hand in and raise towards temple.
3. Elbows	Elbows remain close to body, pointing toward the ground
4. Foot	Slight pivot of foot to allow hip and torso rotation
5. Torso	Turn hips slightly to rotate torso and the same direction the punch is being thrown to absorb the uppercut with the guard
6. Stance	Return to MMA stance

Picture

Your Notes:

Lead Upper Cut

Description: The lead uppercut is a component skill that is most effectively thrown in proximity of the opponent. The lead uppercut, a powerful technique by itself, can also be used to set up other strikes like a cross. Leading with the lead uppercut can be dangerous as it exposes the martial artist's head and opens them to counters.

1. Stance	All elements of MMA Stance in place
2. Hips	Turn hips to shift weight to the front foot
3. Foot	Pivot on rear foot
4. Hips	Hips turn to shift weight to rear foot
5. Hand	As weight shifts to rear foot with hip movement, lead fist is propelled in an upward trajectory
6. Arm	Arm position at approximately 90 degrees through upper cut technique
7. Stance	Return to MMA Stance

Pictures

Your Notes:

MMA Clinch

Description: In MMA the clinch is different than wrestling or Muay Thai. The clinch sets up a variety of strikes and takedowns. The MMA clinch should be used to push and pull the opponent to keep them off balance. This sets up strikes and prevents them from attempting their own offense.

1. Position	Begin with a underhook
2. Collar tie	Use opposite hand to collar tie
3. Head	Forehead pressed into opponent's head facing ear and neck
4. Arms	Underhook and collar tie are used to push and pull opponent off balance

Pictures

Your Notes:

Mount Escape

Description: Being mounted in MMA is one of the worst positions a martial artist can be in. The mount escape is a basic high percentage escape from being mounted.

1. Position	Prone with opponent in full mount
2. Hands	Guard high to defend strikes
3. Head	Off the map
4. Feet	Flat on ground with knees pointed up
5. Hips	Bridge hips high to displace the opponent's balance
6. Arm	Reach from the inside out to trap an arm
7. Leg	Use same side leg to trap opponent's foot with heal
8. Bridge	Bridge, reach with opposite arm and roll at a 45 degree angle
9. Position	Finish in opponent's guard

Pictures

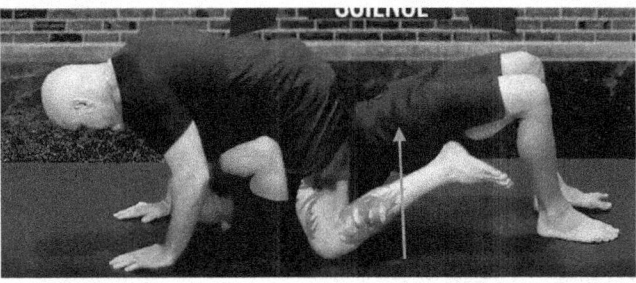
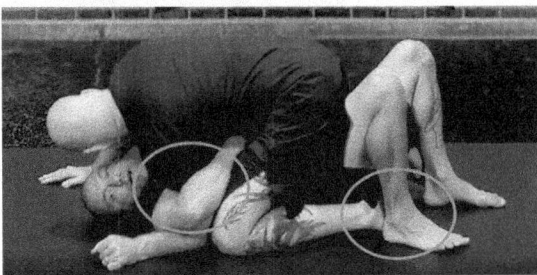

Your Notes:

Outside Low Kick Defense

Description: Leg kicks left unchecked can render the martial artist helpless on their feet. The most important component of this outside low kick is to be in a good stance with knees built. Sometimes the defense can be as easy as stepping forward to "jam" the kick.

1. Stance	All elements of MMA stance in place
2. Footwork	Using linear foot work step forward to "jam" the kick
3. Variation knee	Using linear footwork, step forward lifting knee approximately waist high
4. Foot	Turn foot out towards kick
5. Stance	Return to MMA stance

Pictures

Your Notes:

Outside Low kick

Description: This kick is a high frequency low risk strike with moderate damage that when accrued can do great damage to the opponent. It can also be used as a set up for other offensive techniques.

1. Stance	All elements of MMA Stance in place.
2. Footwork	Lead foot steps forward approximately 45 degrees
3. Jab	Jab is thrown simultaneously as foot steps forward
4. Rear hand	Rear hand frames
5. Rear foot	Push off the ball of the rear foot
6. Knee	Drive knee forward and up
7. Hips	Swing hips approximately 160 degrees
8. Leg	Striking leg swings slightly down with toes flexed up
9. Lead foot	Pivots with hip motion approximately 160 degrees

Pictures

Your Notes:

Outside Trip

Description: Outside leg trip is a high percentage take down in MMA. It is important use the overhook and outside leg to drive forward with momentum to drive the opponent to the ground.

1. Position	Begin from the over-under position
2. Underhook	Pull the opponent forward with the underhook
3. Knees	Bend knees to lower hips below opponents
4. Rear Foot	Push off back foot to create forward momentum into opponent
5. Lead foot	Penetrate lead foot as deep as possible between opponents' legs
6. Hands	With elbows pressed tight slide hands behind the opponents back
7. Grip	Finish hand motion in grip
8. Lead leg	Step the lead leg forward to press tightly behind opponents until the ball of the lead foot is on ground
9. Hooks	Pull the over hooked arm toward the ground, push the underhook up to displace the opponent's balance as chest pushes forward driving opponent to the ground
10. Position	Finish in side mount with hips down, chest up, hands posted on the ground

Pictures

Your Notes:

Pivoting

Description: Pivoting is a fundamental technique has it allows the martial artist to position themselves to effectively utilize defensive and offensive techniques. The critical aspect related to the pivot is remaining squared to the opponent.

1. Stance	All elements of the MMA stance in place
2. Lead foot	Lead foot steps laterally
3. Rear foot	Rear foot swings laterally
4. Pivot	Lead foot pivots
5. Stance	Return to MMA stance.

Picture

Your Notes:

Rear Naked Choke Defense

Description: The rear naked choke is one of the highest percentage submissions attempted to finished in MMA. As such, it is important to be able to effectively defend. A critical

1. Position	Begin with opponent in back mount
2. Shoulders	Shrug shoulders and tuck chin with hands positioned high and close to head
3. Elbow	Pinch elbow tight on underhook
4. Outside Hand	When opponent releases seatbelt, grip the choking wrist to block choke using the hand opposite to that of the opponent
5. Inside Hand	Using the opposite hand, grip same arm (two grips one arm). Elbows remain tight to body
6. Hip	Rotate body to hip on the opposite side of choke
7. Foot	Using the foot that is opposite to that of the hip on the ground, trap the opponent's foot to the ground and slide knee through small gap between the opponent's legs
8. Back	Back positioned flat to the foot
9. Bridge	Elbow to the ground, see the bridge, reach and roll
10. Position	Finish in opponents guard

Pictures

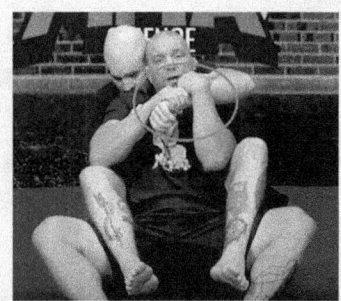

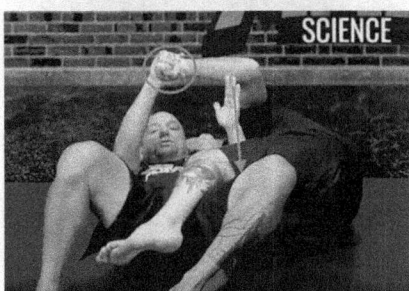
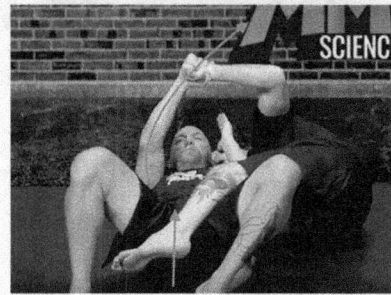

Your Notes:

Rear Naked Choke

Description: This is one of the highest percentage finishes in MMA.

1. Position	Begin from the back mount
2. Grip	Release bottom hand grip
3. Top hand	Shoot same hand as deep as possible over the opponent's shoulder and grip it
4. Elbow	Tip of elbow is in line with chin
5. Chin	Place chin on hand that is gripping shoulder
6. Head	Press head ear to ear with opponent
7. Hand	Slide arm up to make gable grip with elbow pulled in towards the center of the opponent's back
8. Chest	Pull shoulder blades together and simultaneously push chest forward into the opponent's back
9. Elbows	Squeeze elbows inward to finish the choke

Pictures

Your Notes:

GREEN BELT

Rear Uppercut

Description: The rear uppercut is a component skill that is most effectively thrown in proximity of the opponent. The rear uppercut, a powerful technique by itself, can also be used to set up other strikes like a cross. Leading with the rear uppercut can be dangerous as it exposes the martial artist's head and opens them to counters.

1. Stance	All elements of MMA Stance in place
2. Hips	Turn hips to shift weight to the front foot
3. Foot	Pivot on rear foot
4. Hips	Hips turn to shift weight to rear foot
5. Hand	As weight shifts to rear foot with hip movement, rear fist is propelled in an upward trajectory
6. Arm	Arm position at approximately 90 degrees through upper cut technique
7. Stance	Return to MMA Stance

Pictures

Your Notes:

Rear Uppercut Defense	
Description. This fundamental defense to the uppercut requires a good MMA stance.	
1. Stance	All elements of the MMA Stance in place
2. Hands	Using a fist or open palm, pull hand in and raise towards temple.
3. Elbows	Elbows remain close to body, pointing toward the ground
4. Foot	Slight pivot of foot to allow hip and torso rotation
5. Torso	Turn hips slightly to rotate torso and the same direction the punch is being thrown to absorb the uppercut with the guard
6. Stance	Return to MMA stance

Pictures	Your Notes:

Snap Down

Description: The snap down is a fundamental grappling movement that allows the martial artist to transition the opponent from a stand up position to a dominant grappling position on the ground. The key to this technique is using tight pressure and pulling the opponent forward with arms while simultaneously creating pressure in the opposite direction.

1. Position	Begin from the MMA Clinch
2. Legs	Step back with both legs
3. Arms	Using both arms pull the opponent towards ground
4. Collar tie	Release collar tie and grip and pull opponents chin forward with same hand elbow tight to head
5. Underhook	Release underhook and grip opponent's tricep and pull foreword with same hand with elbow pressed toward body
6. Shoulder	Shoulder on side cupping chin drives into middle of opponent's shoulder blade with elbow pressed toward head, and ear on shoulder
7. Feet	On ball of feet driving body forward into opponent
8. Hips	Hips raised at approximately 45 degree to create downward pressure

Pictures

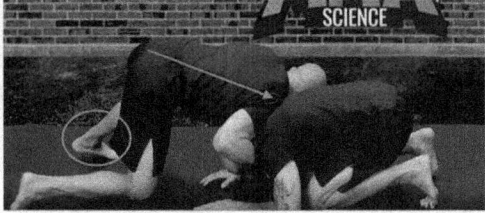

Your Notes:

Standing Guillotine

Description: This is a basic submission is simple choke that occurs from the front head lock position. The critical behavior here is to drive the elbow down while squeezing and rotating the hips and torso back to finish the choke.

1. Stance	All elements in MMA stance
2. Hand	Punch hand through the front headlock position so that the side of the wrist is underneath the opponent's chin
3. Rear foot	No thumb grip with two middle fingers on the bone of the wrist of the arm that is punched through the headlock
4. Hips	Pull opponent close by walking hips forward and pulling both elbows in tight to body
5. Rear hand	Push chest and chin tight to the opponent's back
6. Torso	Posture torso up
7. Arm	Rotate elbow down ("bicep in mirror) and towards inside of the body as squeezing arm into opponent's neck

Pictures

Your Notes:

Switch Lead Kick (Round House)

Description: Round house kicks are powerful. The switch round house allows the martial artist to generate more power by momentarily switching to load the lead kick from the rear.

1. Stance	All elements of the MMA stance in place
2. Switch step	All elements of switch step in place
3. Knee	All elements of straight knee in place
4. Kick	All elements of the rear round kick in place
5. Stance	Return to MMA Stance

Pictures

Your Notes:

Switch Knee	
Description. This is a great technique and improved upon the straight knee because you can change angles. It can be an effective counter to an advancing opponent.	
1. Stance	All elements of the MMA stance in place
2. Switch step	All elements of switch step in place
3. Knee	All elements of straight knee in place
4. Stance	Return to MMA stance.

Pictures

Your Notes:

Switch Snap Kick

Description: While less powerful than round kicks, the switch snap kick generates more power the front snap kick because of the velocity that can be generated from the switch motion. Speed and snap are critical to the success of this technique.

1. Position	All elements of the MMA Stance in place.
2. Switch knee	All elements of switch knee in place
3. Rear leg	Shifts forward, all element of front kick in place
4. Front kick	All elements of lead leg front kick in place
5. Position	Return to MMA stance

Pictures

Your Notes:

Switch Step

Description: The switch step is an important technique for advancing, retreating, and acting on angles.

1. Stance	All elements of MMA Stance in place
2. Lead foot	Push off the ball of the lead foot and switch it to the rear
3. Rear foot	Simultaneously switch rear foot to the lead with the foot angle at approximately 45 degrees
4. Step	Step foot forward from rear to lead
5. Stance	Return to MMA stance

Pictures

Your Notes:

GREEN BELT

45 Step	Yes	No
Target		
1. Stance		
2. Hands		
3. Rear Foot		
4. Lead Foot		
5. Positioning		
6. Stance		
7.		
8.		
9.		
10.		
Percentage Correct	%	

Back Mount Position	Yes	No
Target		
1. Position		
2. Feet		
3. Arms		
4. Hands		
5. Positioning		
6. Head		
7.		
8.		
9.		
10.		
Percentage Correct	%	

Front Head Lock Positioning	Yes	No
Target		
1. Position		
2. Inside Arm		
3. Lead Hand		
4. Elbow		
5. Rear hand		
6.		
7.		
8.		
9.		
10.		
Percentage Correct	%	

Your Notes:

Guillotine from the Guard Defense	Yes	No
Target		
1. Position		
2. Hips		
3. Shoulder		
4. Hand		
5. Head		
6. Hand		
7. Position		
8.		
9.		
10.		
Percentage Correct	%	

Guillotine from the Guard	Yes	No
Target		
1. Position		
2. Legs		
3. Hand		
4. Grips		
5. Elbows		
6. Chest		
7. Torso		
8. Elbow		
9.		
10.		
Percentage Correct	%	

Inside Low Kick Defense	Yes	No
Target		
1. Stance		
2. Lead foot		
3. Knee		
4. Knee variation		
5. Foot		
6.		
7.		
8.		
9.		
10.		
Percentage Correct	%	

Your Notes:

Inside Low Kick			Inside Trip			Lead Upper Cut Defense		
Target	Yes	No	Target	Yes	No	Target	Yes	No
1. Stance			1. Position			1. Stance		
2. Switch Stance			2. Underhook			2. Hands		
3. Hand			3. Leg			3. Elbows		
4. Rear Foot			4. Rear foot			4. Foot		
5. Knee			5. Lead foot			5. Torso		
6. Hips			6. Hips			6. Stance		
7. Lead foot			7. Lead foot			7.		
8.			8. Knee			8.		
9.			9. Hooks			9.		
10.			10. Position			10.		
Percentage Correct		%	Percentage Correct		%	Percentage Correct		%

Your Notes:

Lead Upper Cut			MMA Clinch			Mount Escape		
Target	Yes	No	Target	Yes	No	Target	Yes	No
1. Stance			1. Position			1. Position		
2. Hips			2. Collar tie			2. Hands		
3. Foot			3. Head			3. Head		
4. Hips			4. Arms			4. Feet		
5. Hand			5.			5. Hips		
6. Arm			6.			6. Arm		
7. Stance			7.			7. Leg		
8.			8.			8. Bridge		
9.			9.			9. Position		
10.			10.			10.		
Percentage Correct		%	Percentage Correct		%	Percentage Correct		%

Your Notes:

GREEN BELT

Outside Low Kick Defense			Outside Low kick			Outside Trip		
Target	Yes	No	Target	Yes	No	Target	Yes	No
1. Stance			1. Stance			1. Position		
2. Footwork			2. Footwork			2. Underhook		
3. Variation knee			3. Jab			3. Knees		
4. Foot			4. Rear hand			4. Rear Foot		
5. Stance			5. Rear foot			5. Lead foot		
6.			6. Knee			6. Hands		
7.			7. Hips			7. Grip		
8.			8. Leg			8. Lead leg		
9.			9. Lead foot			9. Hooks		
10.			10.			10. Position		
Percentage Correct		%	Percentage Correct		%	Percentage Correct		%

Your Notes:

Pivoting			Rear Naked Choke Defense			Rear Naked Choke		
Target	Yes	No	Target	Yes	No	Target	Yes	No
1. Stance			1. Position			1. Position		
2. Lead foot			2. Shoulders			2. Grip		
3. Rear foot			3. Elbow			3. Top hand		
4. Pivot			4. Outside Hand			4. Elbow		
5. Stance			5. Inside Hand			5. Chin		
6.			6. Hip			6. Head		
7.			7. Foot			7. Hand		
8.			8. Back			8. Chest		
9.			9. Bridge			9. Elbows		
10.			10. Position			10.		
Percentage Correct		%	Percentage Correct		%	Percentage Correct		%

Your Notes:

Rear Uppercut			Rear Uppercut Defense			Snap Down		
Target	Yes	No	Target	Yes	No	Target	Yes	No
1. Stance			1. Stance			1. Position		
2. Hips			2. Hands			2. Legs		
3. Foot			3. Elbows			3. Arms		
4. Hips			4. Foot			4. Collar tie		
5. Hand			5. Torso			5. Underhook		
6. Arm			6. Stance			6. Shoulder		
7. Stance			7.			7. Feet		
8.			8.			8. Hips		
9.			9.			9.		
10.			10.			10.		
Percentage Correct		%	Percentage Correct		%	Percentage Correct		%

Your Notes:

Standing Guillotine			Switch Lead Kick (Round House)			Switch Knee		
Target	Yes	No	Target	Yes	No	Target	Yes	No
1. Stance			1. Stance			1. Stance		
2. Hand			2. Switch step			2. Switch step		
3. Rear foot			3. Knee			3. Knee		
4. Hips			4. Kick			4. Stance		
5. Rear hand			5. Stance			5.		
6. Torso			6.			6.		
7. Arm			7.			7.		
8.			8.			8.		
9.			9.			9.		
10.			10.			10.		
Percentage Correct		%	Percentage Correct		%	Percentage Correct		%

Your Notes:

GREEN BELT

Switch Snap Kick			Switch Step					
Target	Yes	No	Target	Yes	No	Target	Yes	No
1. Position			1. Stance			1.		
2. Switch knee			2. Lead foot			2.		
3. Rear leg			3. Rear foot			3.		
4. Front kick			4. Step			4.		
5. Position			5. Stance			5.		
6.			6.			6.		
7.			7.			7.		
8.			8.			8.		
9.			9.			9.		
10.			10.			10.		
Percentage Correct		%	Percentage Correct		%	Percentage Correct		%

Your Notes:

Switch Snap Kick			Switch Step					
Target	Yes	No	Target	Yes	No	Target	Yes	No
1.			1.			1.		
2.			2.			2.		
3.			3.			3.		
4.			4.			4.		
5.			5.			5.		
6.			6.			6.		
7.			7.			7.		
8.			8.			8.		
9.			9.			9.		
10.			10.			10.		
Percentage Correct		%	Percentage Correct		%	Percentage Correct		%

Your Notes:

Total Performance Scorecard				
	Skills Passed	Yes	No	Notes
Striking	45_Step			
	Inside low kick			
	Lead uppercut			
	Outside low kick			
	Pivoting			
	Rear uppercut			
	Switch Round house kick			
	Switch knee			
	Switch Snap			
	Switch step			
	Inside low kick defense			
	Rear uppercut defense			
	Lead uppercut defense			
	Outside low kick defense			
Grappling	Back mount position			
	Guillotine from the guard			
	Inside trip			
	Rear naked choke			
	Standing guillotine			
	Front head lock			
	MMA Clinch			
	Outside trip			
	Snap down			
	Front head lock			
	Guillotine from the guard defense			
	Mount Escape			
	Rear naked choke defense			
	Total	%	Scoring Criteria: 80%>=Pass 79%-60%=Eligible for Retest >59%=fail	

Green Belt Criteria Met: [ ] Yes [ ] No

If no, eligible for retest? [ ] Yes [ ] No

REFERENCES

Alessi, G. (1987). Generative strategies and teaching for generalization. *The Analysis of Verbal Behavior*, *5*, 15–27. https://doi.org/10.1007/BF03392816

Allison, M. G., & Ayllon, T. (1980). Behavioral coaching in the development of skills in football, gymnastics, and tennis. *Journal of Applied Behavior Analysis*, *13*(2), 297–314. https://doi.org/10.1901/jaba.1980.13-297

Bandura, A. (1997). *Self-efficacy. The exercise of control*. Freeman and Company.

Binder, C. (1996). Behavioral fluency: Evolution of a new paradigm. *The Behavior Analyst*, *19*(2), 163–197. https://doi.org/10.1007/BF03393163

Boyer, E., Miltenberger, R. G., Batsche, C., & Fogel, V. (2009). Video modeling by experts with video feedback to enhance gymnastics skills. *Journal of Applied Behavior Analysis*, *42*(4), 855–860. https://doi.org/10.1901/jaba.2009.42-855

Brobst, B., & Ward, P. (2002). Effects of public posting, goal setting, and oral feedback on the skills of female soccer players. *Journal of Applied Behavior Analysis*, 35(3), 247–257. https://doi.org/10.1901/jaba.2002.35-247

Edmonds, W. A., Johnson, M. B., Tenenbaum, G., & Kamata, A. (2012). Idiosyncratic measures in sport. In G. Tenenbaum, R. C. Eklund, & A. Kamata (Eds.), *Measurement in Sport and Exercise Psychology* (pp. 81-90). Champaign, IL: Human Kinetics.Gavoni, P., & Gomez, F. (2014). If styles make fights, what makes styles? A break down of style characteristics in fighting part I. *Scifighting Online Magazine*. http://www.scifighting.com/2014/07/18/30856/styles-make-fights-makes-styles-break-style-characteristics-fighting-part

Gavoni, P., & Polk, K. (2018) Fight science: Overcoming fear and anxiety through action. Bloody Elbow

Gavoni, P., & Weatherly, N. (2019). *Deliberate coaching: A toolbox for accelerating teacher performance.* Learning Science International.

Georgiou, A. V. (2008). Pankration – A historical look at the original mixed-martial arts competition. *Black Belt Magazine*, April, 92–97. https://cdn.initial-website.com/proxy/apps/shai10/uploads/gleichzwei/instances/946F8199-B018-4889-B03B-DAEF93CE5D0F/wcinstances/epaper/c124b812-6153-452b-ad8d-793c20abdbf4/pdf/What-is-Pankration-A.-Georgiou-Article-Black-Belt-Magazine-4_2008.pdf

Johnson, K. R., & Chase, P. N. (1981). Behavior analysis in instructional design: A functional typology of verbal tasks. *The Behavior Analyst*, 4(2), 103–121. https://doi.org/10.1007/bf03391859

Krukauskas, F., Miltenberger, R., & Gavoni, P. (2019). Using auditory feedback to improve striking for mixed martial artists. *Behavioral Interventions*, 34, 419–428. https://doi.org/10.1002/bin.1665

Hazen, A., Johnstone, C., Martin, G. L., & Srikameswaran, S. (1990). A videotaping feedback package for improving skills of youth competitive swimmers. *The Sport Psychologist*, 4(3), 213–227. https://doi.org/10.1123/tsp.4.3.213

Knowles, S., Marshall, S., Bowling, J., Loomis, D., Millikan R., Yang, J., & Mueller, F. (2009). Risk factors for injury among high school football players. *Epidemiology*, 20(2), 302–310. https://doi.org/10.1097/EDE.0b013e318193107c

Libby, M. E., Weiss, J. S., Bancroft, S., & Ahearn, W. H. (2008). A comparison of most-to-least and least-to-most prompting on the acquisition of solitary play skills. *Behavior Analysis in Practice*, 1(1) 37–43. https://doi.org/10.1007/BF03391719

REFERENCES

Luiselli, J. K., Woods, K. E., & Reed, D. D. (2011). Review of sports performance research with youth, collegiate, and elite athletes. *Journal of Applied Behavior Analysis*, *44*(4), 999–1002. https://doi.org/10.1901/jaba.2011.44-999

Miltenberger, R. G. (2008). *Behavior modification: Principles and procedures* (4th ed.). Wadsworth.

Polk, K., Schoendorff, B., Webster, M., & Olaz, F. (2016). *The essential guide to the ACT matrix: A step-by-step approach to using the ACT matrix model in clinical practice*. Context Press.

Tradition: Definition of Tradition by Lexico. (n.d.). Retrieved from https://www.lexico.com/en/definition/tradition

Quintero, L. (2018). *Behavioral skills training to teach correct heading skills to youth soccer players* (Master's thesis, University of Southern Mississippi). https://aquila.usm.edu/masters_theses/362

Seniuk, H. A., Witts, B. N., Williams, W. L., & Ghezzi, P. M. (2013). Behavioral coaching. *The Behavior Analyst*, *36*(1), 167–172. https://doi.org/10.1007/bf03392301

Stokes, J. V., Luiselli, J. K., & Reed, D. D. (2010). A behavioral intervention for teaching tackling skills to high school football athletes. *Journal of Applied Behavior Analysis*, *43*(3), 509–512. https://doi.org/10.1901/jaba.2010.43-509

Vargas, E. A., & Fraley, L. E. (1984). Teachers and students: Reflections on social control and future performance. *The Behavior Analyst*, *7*(2), 131–137. https://doi.org/10.1007/bf03391896

PAUL GAVONI

An expert in human performance, coaching, and organizational leadership, Dr. Paul "Paulie" Gavoni is a behavior scientist who has worked in education and human services for over two decades. In this capacity, he served the needs of children and adults in a variety of positions including: COO, Director of School Improvement, Leadership Director, Professor, Assistant Principal, School Turnaround Manager, Clinical Coordinator, Therapist, and Behavior Analyst. As Vice President of Organizational Leadership at Brett DiNovi & Associates, Dr. Gavoni is passionate about applying Organizational Behavior Management (OBM) strategies to establish positive environments and engaging environments.

Beyond his work in education and human services, Dr. Gavoni is also a former fighter and highly respected coach in combat sports. Coach "Paulie Gloves," as he is known in the Mixed Martial Arts (MMA) community, has trained world champions and UFC vets using technologies rooted in the behavioral sciences. Coach Paulie has been featured in the books Beast: Blood, Struggle, and Dreams at the Heart of Mixed Martial Arts, A Fighter's Way, and the featured article Ring to Cage: How four former boxers help mold MMA's finest. He is also an author who has written extensively for a variety of online magazines such as Bloody Elbow, Scifighting, Last Word on Sports, and Bloody Elbow where his Fight Science series continues to bring behavior science to MMA.

Known for his authenticity and practical approaches, Dr. Gavoni is a sought-out speaker at a variety Educational and Behavior Analytic Conferences. Co-author of Quick Wins! Accelerating School Transformation through Science, Engagement, and Leadership, and Deliberate Coaching: A Toolbox for Accelerating Teacher Performance, he is proud to introduce OBM to the massive audience of educators through his numerous publications. His current book in development is titled Behavioral Karma: The 5 Laws of Life and Leadership.

DAVID ZITNICK

David Zitnick has been an athlete all of his life. His passion for developing his overall health and fitness started very early. David began playing organized sports at the age of 6 and started Boxing through the P.A.L. during high school. When high school came to an end David discovered the sport of MMA & has dedicated the last 20 years to improving his skills as a pro MMA fighter and coach. MMA has taken David all over the U.S. and Europe for fights and training. David began training MMA in 2000 had his first Pro fight in 2001.

David began training with Mike Lee (F2 arena/Jungle MMA) in Gainesville, FL. After moving back to South Florida in 2002 David found his home at American Top Team and has been there ever since. David has always loved the striking arts and began training Exclusively with Roger Krahl. After 11 years of training David earned his Black belt in MMA Striking.

David is the Co-founder of MMA Science LLC. MMA Science is bringing tradition, science and organization to MMA. Through the first ever International Belt Ranking system and curriculum based on the science of human behavior. MMA Science is looking to revolutionize the way MMA is taught around the world. David continues to train along-side of each of his students and fighters. David is always seeking out new knowledge to improve his coaching skill set. 20 years of experience will be shared right here!

ROGER KRAHL

Roger is the owner and head trainer at American Top Team of Sunrise. Roger has been involved in the martial arts since 1981 when he started competing on the sport karate circuit in the Northeast. He went on to move to South Florida in 1992 and was co-owner of East West Karate which at the time was the largest dojo in the United States with 1000 active students. After many state & national titles in sport karate it was time to try a new sport. Roger was a member of the WAKO USA kickboxing team and he won the US OPEN in continuous kickboxing in 1998 & 2000. Before American Top Team was founded in 2001, Roger was partners in the first ever MMA academy in South Florida in 1996. It was there that he found a passion for MMA.

Roger partnered with a well known Judoka from Brazil. Alex Davis who was responsible for bringing most of the fighters from Brazil in the early days of the UFC. Olympiad Training Center was born and would boast bringing Marco Ruas (UFC Heavyweight Champion), Pedro Rizzo and Rolles Gracie to coach. Unfortunately this academy would not be as successful financially and had to close the doors in 1999. In 2000, Roger opened up a small academy in Sunrise, Florida and would continue to evolve as MMA was just gaining momentum as its own sport. In 2004, Ultimate Martial Arts would become one of the first American Top Team affiliate academies in South Florida. Roger worked closely with Ricardo Liborio to develop the first ever MMA curriculum for school owners. Coming from a traditional martial arts background, Roger knew how to organize and break down all of the striking techniques that would be used in MMA.

This was our first attempt in breaking down and organizing MMA into a true curriculum. Coming from a karate background also made Roger want to see more of the traditions of martial arts become practiced in this modern day of MMA. Since joining ATT, Roger has trained fighters to World Championships in M-1 Global, Bellator and the UFC. His most famous fighter is considered by many the greatest female fighter of all time. Roger coached Amanda Nunes when she joined ATT and was in her corner when she destroyed Ronda Rousey in just 48 seconds. Roger was considered one of the best MMA striking coaches at American Top Team Headquarters training the top athletes in the sport for the last decade. Since leaving the main academy in September, 2018, Roger has focused on his own academy and developing the MMA Science brand into a global force. We not only want to be the first ever global belt ranking system for MMA, we also want to be the Best!

W. ALEX EDMONDS

Alex Edmonds, PhD, BCB, is currently an associate professor of research at Nova Southeastern University in Davie, Florida. He graduated from Florida State University and received his doctoral degree in Educational Psychology with a minor in Statistics and Measurement. Over the years, Dr. Edmonds has applied his knowledge of research design, measurement and assessment in both field and laboratory examinations. He has published extensively in a variety of areas such as research design, psychophysiology and sport psychology. Prior to graduate school, he was strength and conditioning coach working with professional athletes in football, track, and boxing. He then combined his passion for the sports with the field of psychology making it the emphasis of his graduate work. While in graduate school, he conducted his field work with the track and field team at Florida State and started using biofeedback for research and practice during this time. He has utilized biofeedback extensively with various types of athletes (from golfers to MMA fighters) for performance enhancement, as well as stress-regulation techniques. Dr. Edmonds is certified through the Biofeedback Certification International Alliance in general biofeedback.